Cooking for Adventurers

Cooking for Adventurers

Culinary Adventures for Those Who Just Want to Eat

Bob Wilkins

COOKING FOR ADVENTURERS
CULINARY ADVENTURES FOR THOSE WHO JUST WANT TO EAT

iUniverse books may be ordered through booksellers or by contacting:

iUniverse
1663 Liberty Drive
Bloomington, IN 47403
www.iuniverse.com
1-800-Authors (1-800-288-4677)

ISBN: 978-1-4917-7973-6 (sc)
ISBN: 978-1-4917-7974-3 (e)

Print information available on the last page.

iUniverse rev. date: 10/19/2015

For Kimberley. . .

This book is dedicated to all of my family and friends who have eaten my cooking and gone on to live normal lives. . .

Contents

This book was written neither by, nor for, chefs. In fact, much of what is contained herein would probably send a classically trained chef into a full-blown cardiac infarction.

Though there *are* recipes and methods, this is *not* a cookbook. There are few all-inclusive charts or graphs, no nutritional estimations, no ingredients you need a dictionary to explain or a loan to finance, and all pretentiousness has been boiled away. If I mean 'fry', I will say 'fry'. The reason for all of this is that I've always hated cookbooks, due in no small part to their similarity to textbooks. They tell you what to put together and how to do it, but they don't tell you *why*. Sometimes they try to tell you how easy it is to fit cooking into your day. I will not presume to do so. How you fit anything into your life is your business. I will help as much as I can, but the decision is ultimately yours. Besides, cooking isn't something that we need to *fit* into our lives. Ever since the first person jammed a stick through something resembling meat and held it over a fire, cooking has always been a *part* of life.

I have a passion for cooking. That does not mean that I now or have ever harbored a desire to be a professional chef. Cooking is an expression of creativity, which implies that it is an art form. Thus, I am a hobbyist. I play. I seldom use recipes, and when I do I can never leave them alone. Like any other art form, cooking is nuanced; the personality of the artist shows through in the work and no two pieces are exactly the same. I came about all the recipes in this book by experimentation. You can try them as they are, but it's always fun to play.

We are all adventurers, to a degree, and the facets of our lives dictate the choices we make, whether good or bad. If you're out in the wilderness, you may settle for the energy bars you have in your emergency pack or you could take a chance at fishing, using some of those bars as bait. If you're shuttling four kids around for after-school activities, cooking a four-course meal isn't exactly feasible, but with the proper imagination, you can make a quick meal at home that is as portable as you need, while being a much better health choice than the drive-thru. The one commonality is ingenuity. You work with what you have at hand.

The alert eye will notice that I spend very little time saying anything about special equipment. The main reason for this is *you don't really need it*! One of the biggest excuses people carry with them for not accomplishing goals (besides time) is the lack of equipment. It's easy to say "I couldn't lose weight because I couldn't afford exercise equipment", when it would be just as easy to do pull-ups and push-ups and take up jogging. The same holds true for cooking. Some of

Bob Wilkins

the best compliments I've ever received for my cooking have been over an open fire, on a grill, or from a single pan. You will see this as we progress through the book. First, we will talk about cooking when you have *everything*, and then we will talk about cooking when you have next to *nothing*.

Adventurers adapt. They are survivors. They see advantage and bounty in places that are bleak and daunting. Try out what I've invented here, but don't be afraid to have fun. Tinker and tweak and, more importantly, be creative! Thinking on our feet is a skill that benefits us all in every aspect of life. Whether your next adventure is a trip to the forgotten wilderness or just family game night, knowing how to handle yourself in (or out of) the kitchen will help you survive!

Some Notes on Safety →

The act of cooking can be inherently dangerous, so throughout these pages we will discuss safety as it applies to specific situations, but there are a few things we need to discuss, from the outset:

- **Knives are sharp and other utensils are usually pointed**—Finding part of a finger in their food is not a fun thing for a diner. It's even less fun if you're the person the finger belonged to.
- **Clothing can catch fire, regardless of the type of heat source you are using**—Gas, electric, open flame, etc., will touch off any clothing you are careless enough to drape over it.
- **Putting out a fire means knowing *what kind* of fire it is**—Don't bring water to an oil fight. Smother fires with pan lids or baking soda.
- **Make sure the thing you're cooking is sufficiently *dead***—Some foodstuffs require more cooking than others, because of foodborne pathogens. I've put together a chart on page 16 with the currently held safe temperature ranges. Learn it, live it, love it. . .
- **Keep bugs from spreading**—Cross contamination can happen easily. Do not cut or prep anything using the same surface/utensils with which you sliced or trimmed your protein.
- **Ovens, stovetops, and grills are *hot***—Keep oven mitts and potholders close by and keep body parts away from cooking surfaces. Severe burns can occur even by grazing hot surfaces! Be mindful of what you're doing at all times!

More on that as we go. Let's have some fun. . .

Chapter I

Basics...

And every one that heareth these sayings of mine, and doeth them not, shall be likened unto a foolish man, which built his house upon the sand . . . ~Matthew 7:26

Everyone has to start somewhere. Just as a house needs a good foundation, so too does an adventurer need to know the rudiments of cooking. Basic cooking skills are usually learned when we are young; I learned how to properly fry a hamburger when I was in grade school. If they are attentive, and their parents have the patience to teach them, children may enjoy a nice bit of independence when they grow up and first move out into the world. Preparation or not, this usually happens in one of a couple of ways. Either the fresh, new adventurer moves into his or her first apartment with a plethora of equipment and supplies heaped upon them by various family members, or they move in, unpack partially, bid their goodbyes to those involved in the move, and quickly realize that they couldn't boil a hot dog (if they thought to buy them) because all they have to work with is video game paraphernalia.

Why in the World Would You Cook?

Seriously, it's a legitimate question. Nearly everywhere you go, there are any numbers of places willing to do the cooking for you *and* clean up afterwards. It's certainly an easy choice, as fast food has spread to all corners of the "civilized" world, invading places you wouldn't even have dreamed of. There's a certain worldwide chicken franchise hanging out within sight of the Sphinx! Having someone else do all the work is a time saving option that many are all too happy to entertain, but there are a few drawbacks:

1. **It's not always the healthiest choice.** No, I'm not going to spend time ripping on the fast food industry for their choice of ingredients or the fact that some places have burgers that contain more than three days' worth of calories. Let's just leave it at "not entirely healthy". (It should also be noted that cooking at home is *as healthy as you make it*. If everything

you make is deep-fried or sugar coated, you may still end up buying your doctor a new vacation home.)

2. **It costs money.** Yes, I know cooking on your own costs money too, but making a steak and potato dinner at home is wicked cheap compared to spending twenty bucks or more at a sit-down restaurant. Add to that the fact that your drinks at home are also significantly less, and you've made a major difference in your budget.

3. **Where's the adventure?** Okay, it *is* nice to dine in different places, and you might experience types of food that you haven't encountered before, but the fact remains, the longer you have something done for you, the less able you will be to do it for yourself. I have several friends who wouldn't be able to do anything for themselves if the internet suddenly fell into a black hole. Like any skill, "if you don't use it, you lose it". Or, for that matter, if you never do it, you'll never learn it.

Fast food has done for cooking what video did for radio. Under one roof, fast food has gathered together a group of people and armed them with fryers and bun toasters and a massive array of seasoning choices comprised of mustard, ketchup, and salt, though not necessarily in that order. Occasionally, you may find pepper, but you generally have to ask for it, and it throws them a bit out of whack.

Like many people, my first exposure to true seasoning came from my grandmother's kitchen. The epitome of southern cooking at its finest, she was well-versed in the use of warm spices and peppers, flavoring nearly everything she cooked with a harmonizing blend of earth and fire. Watching her work helped me understand how even the simplest of dishes could carry surprising flavor.

In my college years, I chanced upon a young lady named Madhi, who, during a whirlwind summer, helped ignite my passion for Indian cuisine, with its often pungent and sometimes fiery/sweet flavors. Her vindaloo was the most heavenly plateful of molten lava I had ever tasted. I have spent the many years since attempting to duplicate her Tandoori Chicken, with little success, though I have become quite fluent in curries and the odd Tikka Masala. (It should be noted that, like many "Italian" dishes that actually originated in the United States, legend tells that Tikka Masala originated in an Indian restaurant in the UK.)

Throughout this book, I will speak of spices fleetingly, sharing stories from cooking on the trail to interesting ways to give your soup a bit of a kick. Each recipe you encounter will be laid out, down to the seasonings, but I encourage you to play around with the mixtures. We never truly discover what we enjoy if we just accept what we are given, without putting our spin on things. Toward the end, I have included a list of spices and their most uncommon uses (did you know cayenne pepper will keep rabbits out of your garden, or that ants hate cinnamon?). Let's not get too far ahead of ourselves, though. . .

Before we get started, I suppose we should mention a thing or two about equipment. . .

A Life Less Ordinary or: How I Learned to Stop Smashing Things and Love the Garlic Press—

Whether you are cooking indoors or out, everything in these pages can be done with the most basic collection of cookware and utensils. Buying additional stuff to do the job is completely up to how much work you're willing to do. You may be tired of smashing your garlic with the side of a chef's knife and decide to purchase a garlic press. It makes the job much easier, but have you ever tried to *wash* one? Out of my collection of cookware, I use three main pieces: A large sauté pan, a medium saucepan, and a Dutch oven. As far as utensils, a good-sized spoon and spatula with a decent knife set is all you need to survive. Out of the set, I mostly use the chef's knife, fillet, slicer and paring knife.

Common household knife set (left to right) Chef's Knife, Carving Knife, Fillet Knife, Slicer, Paring Knife, and Serrated Utility

- **Chef's Knife:** The most versatile of the set, this knife chops, slices, dices, and minces.
- **Carving Knife:** This knife's long, thin blade helps cut large pieces of cooked meats.
- **Fillet Knife:** Flexible and sharp, the filet knife is used for trimming fat and deboning fish and poultry.
- **Slicer:** Just as the name implies, this is an "everyday use" knife for slicing cheese, de-crusting the kids' sandwiches, or anything in between.
- **Paring Knife:** A short blade, used for peeling and slicing fruits and veg.
- **Utility:** There are several different types. The one pictured here has a serrated blade for cutting breads and fruit.

While we're on the subject of handy tools, I would like to take this time to express my utter dislike for microwave ovens. Sure, they come in handy for reheating leftovers or warming a quick bowl of canned soup for lunch, but when it comes down to it, it is ridiculously easy to totally dry out and ruin anything you attempt to cook. Even cautiously defrosting foods in the microwave could result in unevenly heated, partially cooked items that, through the magic of high-energy electromagnetic radiation, become quite like shoe leather. There are a few places in the chapters ahead where I freely admit getting lazy and using a microwave oven. Usually, all of these times were necessitated by being exceptionally short on time. Overall, I try to avoid it. If, however, you need hot water in a pinch, or to quickly zap up some beef or chicken bouillon, then by all means, nuke away!

A Note on Ingredients—

You could be the best chef on the planet, with the most advanced and well-equipped kitchen possible, and still only turn out mediocre fare if you have lousy ingredients. While, undoubtedly, you could classify your ingredients in a few thousand different ways, there are, basically, three types of produce:

- Commercially produced
- Farmer's market
- Home-grown

It's no secret that buying commercially produced foods is a crapshoot, from a nutritional standpoint. Thanks to labelling laws, you know approximately where the items you are purchasing came from, but you have no idea what may have happened to it, from its life in the field to hitting your local grocery store's produce section. In fact, you have no real way of knowing just how *long* that journey was, as well. Some foods can be in cold storage *for as long as a year* before coming to your grocer's shelf! Add to that the possibility of pesticide and various biological contaminations, and you end up with the sudden urge to swear off salad completely.

Farmers' Markets are a good alternative to regular grocery stores, inasmuch as you have the potential to get your hands on some fresh food that doesn't give you the heebies. Keep in mind, though, there are a couple of different types. Many farmers' markets are stocked with both locally grown produce and other *domestically* grown items (basically meaning, they shipped in some things that can't easily be grown in that particular area). These markets are usually run by one or two people that you can actually get to know well enough to get the lowdown on where everything has come from. The other type of farmers' market looks the same as the first, but careful inspection will reveal one or two "local" items and a mess of things that come from other parts of the world. You can still get some good items, but pay attention to labelling and be wary of markets where you never see the same people twice.

Home grown vegetables are your first, best choice, in the quest for quality. If you grew it yourself, you know what was used to fertilize the soil, and you should have a good idea which tomato plants your dog peed on. Make no mistake, however; gardens take some work, and take time to nurture. One thing they don't require is a lot of space. You don't need a huge yard to put in a good vegetable garden. I have friends with "postage stamp" yards and even townhomes with no yard at all who have made due with all sorts of planting ideas, from buckets and hanging pots to handmade planters. I'm not going to get into all of the ins and outs here (that will be another book), but if you want to research efficient at-home gardening, there is a litany of information on the web.

Let's face it, there is nothing like a selection of vegetables that came from your own garden. Onions are ridiculously easy to grow in many types of soil. Tomatoes and peppers require a little bit of extra work and maybe some creative fertilizing, but will make for an enjoyable summer project.

On Cooking With Wine—

Cooking with wine does not have to be expensive or difficult. As a rule, I do not purchase expensive wines, as I use them more for cooking than anything else. We do keep a running list of wines we've tried, separating them into "Yes!" and "Dreadful" categories, so as not to repeat any unnecessary mistakes. Wine is a very versatile resource to have at hand for both flavor and health-conscious reasons. It can be used in the sautéing process to reduce the amount of oil you are using, while adding extra flavor (substitute an equal amount of wine for each increment of oil you take out). Sautéing onions and mushrooms in red wine will give them a deep flavor accent that helps along any gravy or stew, again without the fat. Even *cake mixes* can benefit, substituting white wine for oil entirely, giving the cake a lighter texture.

I could go on for an entire chapter yammering about which wines go with what foods. One of my most favorite action movies involved the master spy figuring out who the Russian bad guy was, simply because *he ordered red wine with fish*! It is generally held that red wine goes with red meat (because the tannins in the wine act as a palate cleanser for bolder proteins), and light wines go with light proteins. Except for pork, this goes with either. A good rule of thumb is to just use what you like.

It is also to be noted that, **just because something is thoroughly cooked, doesn't mean the alcohol has been completely evaporated**! Scientifically speaking, alcohol evaporates at 172°F, which means any sauces or gravies you may be simmering should come out fine, with sufficient cook time. Baked or roasted foods can still have between 5-25% of the alcohol remaining, depending on such variables as cook time, exposed surface area, etc. If you find yourself cooking for a recovering alcoholic, small children, or people who, in general, do not cotton to the use of alcohol outside of its medicinal uses, there are several non-alcoholic wines to choose from. Be considerate!

Feeling the Heat—

Knowing how to cook with different types of heat is as important as knowing the food you are using. Electric ranges are slow to heat up and slow to cool. Once you turn off the burner, the heat is still there, meaning you have to move the pan to remove the heat. Another pitfall comes from the fact that the heat conveyance is so complete (from direct contact between the pan and heat source) that plastic utensils will melt very quickly, so you have to avoid the urge to 'drag' against the bottom of the pan while stirring. Gas ranges are very responsive, easily adjustable, and the heat goes away instantly when you shut off the burner. This tends to make gas the way to go for the stovetop. The flip side to this is that gas ovens heat up so quickly compared to electric ones that they can be detrimental to the baking process, requiring temperature adjustments.

Open flame is the most challenging, by far, but it is also the most versatile, as you can cook both directly and indirectly at the same time. Whether on a grill or over a fire pit, both meat and veg alike can be cooked with much finesse and little fuss. With a little practice, you can even bake with open fire, but we can talk about that later!

Beginnings—

When you cook any type of protein with dry heat (sautéing or frying, for example), deposits of caramelized sugars, carbohydrates, and proteins adhere to the bottom of the pan. The name for these is *sucs*, from the French word *sucre* (sugar). After removing the meat, a deglazing liquid such as wine, broth, etc. are added as the pan is returned to the heat. A quick reduction and some seasoning, and you have a *fond* (from the French for *foundation*). This method is the base for many sauces and gravies, and can even be used as a base for soups. The limit is your imagination!

I love barbecue sauce. That's all I can say about it. A properly done barbecue sauce will add life to complex, grilled proteins, sandwiches, and French fries, alike. It has a much better flavor than mere ketchup, and there are so many varieties to choose from that you need never become bored with it. I obsessed over developing my own recipe(s) after trying a rather dreadful version from a TV chef (who shall remain nameless). The resultant cacophony of discordant flavors in that particular recipe could best be described as hell (assuming hell had been flooded with vinegar for Sunday water skiing).

What follows are some sauces, marinades, and gravies that are relatively simple, yet complex enough that they can be used in a multitude of ways, both indoors and out.

Saucier and Saucier—

Basic Barbecue

A simple sauce for simple times, this one works well for grilling and baking poultry and fish!

3 Tbsp. Ketchup
2 Tbsp. Vinegar
1 Tbsp. Lemon Juice
2 Tbsp. Worcestershire Sauce
4 Tbsp. Water
2 Tbsp. Butter
3 Tbsp. Brown Sugar
1 Tsp. Salt
1 Tsp. Yellow Mustard
1 Tsp. Chili Powder
1 Tsp. Paprika

Combine all ingredients and simmer for 30-40 minutes, stirring occasionally.

Korean Barbecue

¼ Cup soy sauce
¼ Cup water
3 Tbsp sugar
2 Tbsp sesame oil (veg oil may be substituted if necessary)
¼ Tsp. ginger
¼ Tsp. pepper
⅛ Tsp. Onion Powder

Whisk together all ingredients in a small saucepan. Bring to a boil and then simmer slowly for five minutes. Allow meat to marinate in a zip-sealed bag for 30 minutes to an hour (the longer you marinate, the more flavor is transferred).

Burgundy Marinade

⅓ Cup Red Wine
¼ Cup Beef Broth
2 Tbsp. Balsamic Vinegar

¼ Tsp. Coarse Black Pepper
3 Garlic Cloves, Minced
1 Tbsp. Brown Sugar

Combine all ingredients and add to a gallon-sized, zip-sealing storage bag with beef (steak or roast). Allow to marinate for 20 minutes to an hour. For steaks, simmer marinade, reducing slightly, and then serve over meat. For roast, use as a fond after the meat is pan-seared, then add reduced sauce to roasting pan.

Marinara Sauce

¼ Cup White Zinfandel
1 Tbsp. Olive Oil
1 small onion, chopped well
2 garlic cloves, pressed or finely chopped
3 Cups diced tomatoes (roughly two 14 oz. cans, if you wish to shortcut)
6 oz. tomato paste
¾ Tsp. Salt
¼ Tsp. Coarse Ground Pepper
2 Tbsp. Chopped Basil
½ Cup Chopped Mushrooms, if desired

- Heat oil in a 4 quart saucepan over medium heat
- Add onion and cook until tender, stirring occasionally
- Stir in garlic and cook one minute
- Stir in tomatoes, wine, tomato paste, salt & pepper
- Heat to boiling over high heat, stirring to break up tomatoes
- Stir in mushrooms
- Reduce heat to medium, stirring occasionally, for fifteen minutes
- Stir in basil

This sauce goes well with any type of pasta, though I've found vermicelli to be the best. In Italy, marinara is only referred to as it associates with other recipes. 'Spaghetti alla marinara' comes out to mean 'mariner's spaghetti'.

The spaghetti dinner is an old 'fallback' for many who find themselves with someone to cook for and no appreciable kitchen experience to speak of. There is little to screw up when all you have to do is boil pasta and heat a jar of sauce.

The true way to impress the family, friends, or special date, however, is to go above and beyond. Sauté a couple of chicken breasts while the sauce is coming to a boil, then add them to the sauce as it simmers. Serve with vermicelli.

Gravies—

Being from a Southern state, gravy has a warm place in my heart. Whether your aim is for a rich, mushroom-laden sauce or a garden-variety biscuit lotion, gravies (when applied properly) have the ability to enhance the flavors of a meal without requiring a chemical engineering level of understanding with regard to spices. The drawback to most gravies is that they are rarely healthy additions to the plate, but there are a few recipes I have stumbled across that won't clog your arteries too badly before you get back to the wilds to work it all off.

Basic Brown Gravy

1 Tbsp. olive oil
1¼ Cup water
¼ Cup red wine (usually a cabernet or burgundy)
¼ Cup flour
1 small onion, chopped
¼ Cup butter
1 Bouillon cube
Salt and Pepper to taste

A variation to this is to just use 1 ½ c of water, if you neither have nor want to use wine. I recommend using a cabernet, though, as it will lend a gentle flavor without overpowering the whole mix.

Sauté the onions in olive oil until tender. Add butter. Once the butter is completely melted, add all the other ingredients except the bullion cube. Toss in the cube once the mixture starts to bubble and stir until completely dissolved. Don't forget to season!

Instead of a bouillon cube, you can also substitute a cup of beef broth for a cup of water

11

Bob Wilkins

Mushroom Gravy

4 oz. can *or* 1 cup fresh mushrooms, chopped
4 minced Garlic Cloves
2 Tbsp. butter
1 chopped onion
½ Cup red wine
1 Tbsp. balsamic vinegar
1 Tbsp. cornstarch dissolved in 1 ½ c cold water
½ Tsp. sugar
Salt and Pepper to taste

Sauté the garlic in butter over low heat, stirring until golden. Remove garlic to a bowl and sauté onion, stirring, until softened. Add mushrooms and increase heat moderately, stirring until thoroughly heated. Add garlic, wine, and vinegar. Bring to a boil until liquid is evaporated. Stir in the cornstarch mixture and sugar and bring to a boil. Reduce heat and simmer for about two minutes, seasoning to taste.

Biscuit Lotion

¼ Cup shortening or bacon grease
2 Cups milk
¼ Cup flour
Salt and Pepper to taste

In a medium size skillet over medium heat, add the shortening or bacon grease and heat slowly. Add the flour and, reducing heat to low, stir vigorously until it is well-combined (a whisk helps here). This usually takes 2-5 minutes. Add the milk ¼ cup at a time, stirring until it is combined with the roux. Keep this up until it reaches the desired thickness, but remember that it will thicken while it stands.

Milk gravy is a staple in southern states and shows up in everything from basic biscuits and gravy to country fried steak. This is a very simple recipe and just begs to be played with. As with many of my concoctions, I like to add a little cayenne pepper, parsley, and (where breakfast is concerned) sausage bits.

Bread—

Bread making can be as easy or as complicated as you want it to be. In the adventuring spirit, we will, of course want the former. As the availability of fast solutions are many, such as ready-made biscuit dough and commercially available breads and rolls, we will not dwell on this too much. I have included a couple of quick and easy recipes here, plus there will be a few more in later chapters.

Basic Biscuits

2 Cups Flour
½ Tsp. Salt
4 Tsp. Baking Powder
2 Tbsp. Shortening
¾ Cup Milk

Sift the dry ingredients and then gently rub in the shortening until it is just blended. With the milk as cold as possible, begin to mix into the flour to form a soft dough. Place the dough on a well-floured table or board and pat down to about ¾ inch thick. Cut into rounds and place them on a baking pan, making sure they do not touch. Bake for 12-14 minutes at 425 degrees.

Dinner Rolls

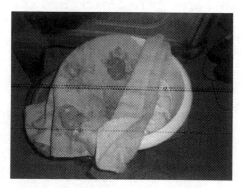

6 Cups Flour
2 Cups Warm Milk
1 Pkg. Dry Yeast (dissolve in the milk)
½ Cup Sugar
¼ Tsp. Salt
1 Egg
¼ Cup Oil

Mix everything together but the flour, then slowly add it as well, kneading as you go. Place in a well-oiled bowl, then cover and set it in a warm place to allow it to rise (to double its size). Roll out the dough and cut into rounds, placing them on an oiled cookie sheet. Cover and let rise again. When they have doubled in size, place in a 400 degree oven until golden brown.

In the winter, we set these next to our buck stove to warm and rise, but you have to watch out! Get them too close to the wood stove and the dough will start cooking in the bowl!

Out in the Wild

Back in my college days, I learned how to make an all-purpose baking mix that can be put together in advance and packed into your site in zip-seal storage bags:

8 Cups All Purpose Flour
½ Cup Powdered Milk
5 Tbsp. Baking Powder
4 Tsp. Salt

Mix well and store until your next outing.

When you get where you're going, take 2 cups of the pre-mix and add 4 Tbsp. butter and then slowly add about ¾ Cup of water. Your objective is stiff biscuit dough. You can pull off pieces of the dough and form them into biscuit shapes to bake in a Dutch oven until golden brown, or make 'doughboys'. A doughboy is made from biscuit dough molded around the end of a stick (usually about ¾ inch diameter or better) and cooked over a warm coal bed, turning to cook evenly. The bread is done when it sounds 'hollow' when tapped with a knife. If your stick is of significant thickness, the cavity left when you slide the bread off is just right for jelly, peanut butter, or even hot dogs!

Chapter II

Meat!

Let's face it. . . Without meat, there would be no cooking. There very well might be baking, but cooking as we know it wouldn't exist. It was a stroke of genius to apply meat to a fire. Or maybe it was an accident, and doing it again was the stroke of genius. However it worked out, though, one thing is for certain: Fire makes good meat. Fire also makes good veg, too, but you have to be very careful. We'll talk about that later.

Cooking meat isn't very difficult once you've had a little practice, though the type of meat dictates how you should treat it, both for taste and even safety issues. In *The Bachelor Home Companion*, P.J. O'Rourke said, "Poultry is like meat, except when you cook it rare. Then it's like bird-flavored Jell-O." While this is a rather revolting thought, it still fails to convey the hideous disgust one feels upon biting into undercooked bird. I have long been a proponent for eating rare meats, but pork and poultry are the definitive 'well-dones' you should always adhere to.

Growing up, I couldn't stand steak; my favorite part of the meal was always the mashed potatoes. The reason for this was my mother and her paranoia with raw meats. She needed to make certain that the steak was completely *dead* and, as you would guess, completely devoid of juices. When I became old enough to go out and order my own steaks, a chance encounter with some rare meat began a very long love affair with bloody beef.

The simplest and best way to cook a steak is also the easiest way to ruin it. Grilling is the most flavorful method, but you have to follow the rules. Your steak must be well-marbled, tender, and not too thick (usually ¾ to 1 inch), as the grill is high and dry heat. Once your coals are ready, they should be raked so that one side of the grill is warmer than the other. Your temperature is correct when you can hold your hand over the hot side for only 2-3 seconds, and 5-6 seconds over the cooler side. The steaks are generally ready to flip when you see beads of blood forming on the top (about 4-6 minutes for 1 inch thick). Once both sides are seared, the steak can be moved to the cooler side of the grill to finish cooking to desired doneness. Letting it rest after cooking allows the juices to return to the center of the steak.

Now, the average adventurer may not always have a grill and firewood/charcoal at their disposal (horrors!), and may have to resort to other means. First off, *frying* is not *sautéing*! Though both are done in a pan with oil (just enough to glaze the pan's bottom), *sautéing* is cooking smaller pieces of food at a medium-high to high heat, using a tool such as a wooden spoon or spatula to keep them moving about the pan to cook evenly. *Frying* involves cooking larger pieces (chicken breasts, steaks, etc.) at a lower heat to cook the food thoroughly without burning it. *Roasting* involves using dry, indirect heat to slowly cook larger cuts of meats. Poultry can also be roasted, as well as potatoes, carrots, and other root vegetables.

Steak is just one of the many forms meat may take, and there are so many ways to make the best of it! Most people think that elaborate meat dishes require hours in the kitchen. Some meals do, but most are simple and easy fare that, once started, does not require a constant eye to ensure perfection.

**A note on doneness. . .

It is impossible to tell whether or not a protein is safely cooked by sight alone! Cooked meats can appear pink, even when a safe internal temperature has been reached (including pork). Making certain your proteins have been cooked to a temperature sufficient to destroy any pathogens (germs) requires the use of a meat thermometer to adhere to the following guidelines:

What is it?	Dangerous Stuff	Safe Internal Temperature (°F)	Rest Time
Ground Meat & Meat Mixtures	Beef, Pork, Veal, Lamb	160	None
	Turkey, Chicken	165	None
Fresh Beef, Veal, Lamb	Steaks, roasts, chops	145	3 minutes
Poultry	Chicken & Turkey, whole	165	None
	Poultry breasts, roasts	165	None

	Poultry thighs, legs, wings	165	None
	Duck & Goose	165	None
	Stuffing (cooked alone or in bird)	165	None
Pork and Ham	Fresh pork	145	3 minutes
	Fresh ham (raw)	145	3 minutes
	Precooked ham (to reheat)	140	None
Eggs & Egg Dishes	Eggs	Cook until yolk and white are firm	None
	Egg dishes	160	None
Leftovers & Casseroles	Leftovers	165	None
	Casseroles	165	None
Seafood	Fin Fish	145 or cook until flesh is opaque and separates easily with a fork.	None
	Shrimp, lobster, and crabs	Cook until flesh is pearly and opaque.	None
	Clams, oysters, and mussels	Cook until shells open during cooking.	None
	Scallops	Cook until flesh is milky white and firm.	None

Now that we've got the boring stuff out of the way, we can dive into the fun stuff. So, you have raw meat. . . Now what?

Beef—

Swiss Steak

The average adventurer may not always be in a position to afford the more tender cuts of beef; therefore knowledge of Swiss steak preparation comes in handy. This is a slow-cooking method to make tougher cuts such as round steak easier to handle.

2 Pounds round or top round steak
1-2 Tbsp. flour

Seasoned pepper, to taste
3 Tbsp. canola oil
1 Onion, rough-chopped
2 Garlic cloves, chopped
2 Cups tomato sauce
6-8 Ounces tomato puree (either homemade or canned)
1 Tsp. dried thyme
1 Tsp. dried basil

Rub flour into the steak and sprinkle seasoned pepper on both sides. Heat a shallow pan coated with 2 Tbsp. of oil, and then brown the steak on both sides. Remove the steak and set it aside. Add the onions and garlic to the pan with another Tbsp. of oil, using a spatula to scrape up the sucs from browning and to keep things moving, so nothing gets scorched. When the garlic turns golden and the onions have started to get tender, add the tomato sauce and puree to the pan and then return the steaks, sprinkling the thyme and basil over everything. Cover and bring to a simmer, reducing heat as low as possible to still maintain a slow simmer. The steak will be cooked through inside of a half hour, but the longer it simmers the more tender it will be. If you have time, push it to an hour. This serves well with mashed potatoes and most any vegetable you like! If you need to increase the amount, add 2 more cups of tomato sauce to up the gravy output; it's great on the potatoes and helps fill up your starving pack of kids!

It should be noted that, when working with a less expensive, leaner cut of beef, that beer (yes, beer!) makes for an excellent marinade. The slightly acidic nature of the brew makes it an excellent tenderizer. Place the meat in a zip-sealed bag and add beer. Marinate for a few hours, or even overnight. Though one may find it wasteful to discard after marinating the beef, the beer has been infused with *raw beef blood*, so you should resist the urge to drink it.

London Broil

London broil refers to the method of preparation, rather than the cut of meat. Traditional London broil is actually a lamb dish, though it can be made with just about any cut of meat you have available. In some parts of Canada, London broil is actually a ground meat patty wrapped in flank steak. *I like this way best:*

½ Cup red wine
¼ Cup soy sauce

¼ Cup water
1 Tbsp. molasses
2 Garlic cloves, chopped
2 pound flank or round steak

Cut both sides of beef in a diamond pattern ⅛ inch deep and place in a shallow baking dish. Mix all other ingredients and pour over steak, marinating 6-8 hours. When ready to cook, discard marinade. Place steak on broiler rack, 2 inches from the heat for 5 minutes on each side, or grill 5-8 minutes per side. Both will get a rare result, or add time for more doneness. Cut the meat into thin slices across the grain at a slanted angle.

Basic Meat Loaf

Ah, meat loaf—such a wonderful little dish with a semi-revolting name! Meat loaf is one of those consistently-remembered comfort foods from our youth. True happiness comes to the adventurer when he or she learns how to duplicate mother's meat loaf. For those less fortunate, here's a couple of ways to try:

2 Pounds ground beef or chuck (the leaner the meat, the less grease you wind up with)
6 Tbsp. Worcestershire sauce
1 Medium onion, finely chopped
1 Cup dry bread crumbs or ½ cup quick oats
2 Eggs
1 Can tomato sauce (or try 1 cup marinara sauce or ¾ cup barbeque sauce!)
½ Tsp. black pepper

Mix everything together, press into a loaf pan and bake for 75 minutes at 350 degrees.

A Loaf Less Ordinary

This recipe is a bit more involved and requires some forethought. The loaf is cooked without a pan, keeping the mixture mostly dry so the meat retains its shape (usually). If you have access to a food processor, your life will be much easier. This method also includes adding a glaze during cooking, which involves not only opening the oven, but working on something already inside it. *This would be an excellent time to remember that the inside of the oven door is exceptionally hot!*

Bob Wilkins

2 Pounds ground chuck
½ Tsp. black pepper
½ Tsp. cayenne pepper
1 Tsp. chili powder
4 Cloves garlic, chopped
1 Small onion, chopped
½ Yellow or red bell pepper (A whole pepper just overruns everything else)
1 Egg
¾ Cup flavored croutons (garlic and butter or cheese and garlic flavor are awesome!)

Glaze—

½ Cup Ketchup
½ Tsp. Garam Masala*
½ Tsp Worcestershire sauce
1-2 drops hot sauce
1 Tbsp. honey

Crush croutons to a fine consistency and mix with spices. Finely chop the garlic, onions, and pepper (if you use a food processor, be certain to not puree the mix, just chop). Combine spice mix and veg in a mixing bowl and mix thoroughly with egg and ground chuck (YES, it is perfectly fine to use your hands. You *did* wash them, didn't you?). Form into a loaf and place on a shallow-sided baking sheet. If, like mine, your baking sheets have given up the 'non-stick' fight, a sheet of parchment paper will keep the loaf from adhering to the metal. Bake at 350 degrees for about 45 minutes. (The glaze gets brushed on after the loaf has been in the oven for about ten minutes or so.)

*Garam Masala is a wonderful little spice that is used in many traditional Indian dishes. It contains cumin; a spice that is used in everything from curries to southwestern fare!

Seasoning meat loaf is an excellent launch pad for other experimentation. When you learn how to comfortably season a meatloaf, seasoning beef for hamburgers becomes second nature. Play with spice blends and even sauces; though don't get too happy with sauce, as your patties won't hold their shape on the grill. Trust me, there's nothing more frustrating than trying to flip goo.

Chicken—

Chicken is, quite possibly, the easiest protein to work with. It can be left whole, cut up, used in stews, curries, spaghetti dishes, baked, or fried countless ways. Basically, if you can put together a handful of ingredients, you can make it complete with chicken. Grilling is especially tricky, as it is easy to overdo the exterior without fully cooking the interior. The best method is to either grill the meat indirectly, or raise the grill higher off the coals than you would have it with beef. The ideal grilling temperature is between 350-375 degrees (See the "Hand Thermometer" detail in the Camping Section). Season the chicken as you like, patting the meat with as much dry seasoning as will stick (some will fall off during grilling, so don't be shy!). Place the meat on the grill, watching for flare-ups from the dripping fat. The pieces will start to become firm, with a nice brown color starting on the bottom. This will be about 15 minutes in at these temperatures. Flip *and rotate* the pieces so that they heat evenly. If the outside is getting done too quickly, move the pieces away from the heat so they will cook slower. 30 minutes in, the chicken is ready for sauce. If you aren't going to add sauce, just cook until done. Otherwise, reduce the grill temp to about 250 degrees (below the point at which sugar ignites) and brush a thick coat of barbeque sauce on the top side of the pieces, closing the lid to cook for 5 minutes. Open the grill, turn the pieces, and brush with sauce. Close the lid and cook for another 5 minutes. This can be repeated until the desired coating is achieved.

Chicken Parmesan

4 Boneless, skinless chicken breasts
2 Eggs
1 Cup bread crumbs
1 Cup parmesan cheese
8 Ounces sliced mozzarella
1 Tsp. dried basil
¼ Cup olive oil
Marinara sauce from page 10
Spaghetti

With marinara sauce simmering, preheat oven to 400 degrees. In a mixing bowl, combine bread crumbs and ½ cup of parmesan. In a separate bowl, whisk the eggs. Heat the oil in a large sauté pan over medium-high heat (the oil should not be smoking). One piece at a time, dredge the chicken through the egg and then the breadcrumbs, and then lay them into the sauté pan, reducing the heat to medium. Gently fry each breast about 3-4 minutes per side. Spread a thick coat of marinara sauce on the bottom of a 9x13 casserole dish or baking pan and arrange the breasts on top. Spoon some sauce on each breast and sprinkle with basil, and then cover each with a slice of mozzarella and the remaining parmesan cheese. Bake until the mozzarella begins to brown. Serve with spaghetti and the remaining sauce.

Korean Barbecue Chicken

6-8 Chicken thighs marinated in Korean barbecue sauce (page 9)
--You can also substitute breasts, drumsticks, or just quarter a whole chicken!

Cook marinated chicken in a 400 degree oven for about 45 minutes (bone-in) or 25-30 minutes (boneless). Grilling is also an option!

Southern-Fried Chicken

Let's face it, in this age of health-paranoia, a large amount of people hear the word 'fried' and instantly begin looking for *Infarction*, the lesser-known Fifth Horseman of the Apocalypse, to come riding out of the sky. Fear not! There are a few simple things you can do to allow for guilt-free enjoyment of this classic fare.

First of all, you need to create the dredge: Step one is usually a combination of egg and buttermilk whisked well in a bowl large enough to soak each piece, individually. If you haven't any buttermilk on hand, put a tablespoon of white vinegar or lemon juice in a measuring cup and fill with milk to the one cup line. Let it stand for about five minutes and you're ready to go! Step two is a bowl with the breading mix. The most common, basic mix is a flour and cornstarch combination. A good mix is ¾ cup flour to 1 Tbsp. cornstarch. If you're cooking a large amount of chicken you may need to increase, but keep in mind that you only want a hint of flour on each piece. (You may want to play with seasoning the breading. I mix cayenne and seasoned pepper in with the flour/cornstarch mix.) After dipping a piece in the buttermilk/egg, dredge it through the flour, coating it on all sides. Tap the pan to knock off any excess flour.

Your oil should be about 350 degrees. After the pieces have been floured, slowly place them in the oil. Some experts will recommend peanut oil, as it has a high smoke-point. Since it has a higher monounsaturated fat content than polyunsaturated, it remains pretty stable when heated, but should only be used occasionally*. Frying in shallow oil will render the fat from the skin, causing it to form a crispy crust. When the pieces are removed from the oil, they should be allowed to drip over the pan for a bit, to drain off the excess oil. If you have a rack, the pieces can continue to drip while the rest cooks. It's much better than the old 'paper towels in the chicken basket' method.

*Polyunsaturated fats are unstable when heated and produce free radicals.

Some Notes on Marination

Occasionally, meats are marinated to both add flavor and tenderize tougher cuts. Marinades can be made from wines, beers, oils, fruit juices, or even colas mixed with other oils and herb/spice blends. The marination process can last for minutes to days, depending on the desired effect, but normally will only be an hour or two at the most. If you are traveling to camp or just grilling at the lake, placing the meat in your choice of marinade in a zip-sealed bag and then dropping it in the cooler before departure is an easy way to go. The acids usually present in the base liquid causes a breakdown of the meat, allowing it to absorb the moisture and flavor. Depending on the type of marinade, soaking red meats for too long can sometimes cause a greying of the tissue, or even break it down to the point that the meat becomes spongy.

Generally, you will just need enough marinade to cover the meat. Larger cuts may require occasional turning, but you should also consider the fact that the marinade is only going to penetrate so far. If you are trying to marinate a fairly large roast, your marinade's flavors will be confined to the outer layers, leaving the center of the cut untouched.

Safety is also a concern when marinating proteins, as raw meats may harbor harmful bacteria that can be transferred to the marinade. Because of this, marination should only be done in the refrigerator, and the only time the marinade can be made into a sauce is if it is brought to the boiling point during the cooking process, as with the Burgundy marinade I mentioned on pages 9-10. If boiling the marinade will ruin its flavor, a simple solution would be to just make some more, skipping the step where you add the raw, bloody meat.

CHAPTER III

The Chemistry of Cooking—
Soups and Stews

Generally, when you think of quick, portable foods, homemade soup rarely comes to mind. In this day and age, when you mention 'food on the go', most people think 'burger', 'wrap', 'burrito', etc. While it is true that most people want something they can easily cram while driving, the experienced adventurer realizes the importance of a relaxing meal break while traveling. One of my most prized possessions is a thermos my grandfather used during his time working Civil Service at Fort Knox, KY. It served him faithfully for many years and has been on several hunting trips with myself and my own children, whether it carried tea, coffee, or our latest mulligan.

The best thing about soups and stews is the fact that they are easier than they look. In its most basic form, soup is just food heated in water with spicy bits mixed in. Soups are comforting and warming. Whether you have just boiled some hastily-caught and cleaned game in a can of water over your survival fire, or put together a hearty beef stew or chili for a family gathering around the table, you will find no better spirit lifter for long, winter nights.

My first solo attempt at soup was inaccurately called 'Mulligan Stew'. It was a simple recipe for a beef stew that I got from a storybook in the third grade which included no more than stew beef, tomato sauce, carrots, onions, and salt and pepper. Since then, I've experimented with so many combinations and concoctions that I have probably forgotten more than I remember. As I said before, though, no two works of art are alike. My beef stew is fundamentally the same each time, though the flavors are subtly different, since I am always playing with spices and methods. Because of their experimental nature, I won't dwell too long on their mechanics, but here are some basics to share (don't forget to check out the 'campfire soup' recipe in the 'Camping' section, too!).

Brunswick Stew

Though the origins are debated, Brunswick stew has been a staple throughout the American South since the 1800's. Tomato-based, it features lima or butter beans and a large variety of choices of meat. There is no 'official' recipe for the stew, but it is, essentially, a thick vegetable soup with meat added. The version I make uses chicken as its primary protein, but I have made it with turkey and, on occasion, even squirrel. I have seen versions of this stew that even use venison or pulled barbeque pork.

When I was a small child, I read a story in which the main character tricked her stingy, old uncle into making enough soup for the whole town using only a button. Whenever my mother made hers, we always made a big deal about 'adding the button'. She did, of course, fish it out before serving, as choking to death on a piece of clothing would have put a damper on the meal, but like the book's recipe, this stew, with its few ingredients, will feed a large family, usually with leftovers.

One whole chicken or 4-6 boneless breasts
32 oz. diced tomatoes
1 Pkg. frozen lima beans
1 Pkg. frozen corn
2 Large onions, chopped
1 Tbsp. butter
3 Slices bread, diced or torn apart
Salt, pepper, and cayenne to taste
8-12 oz. of either egg noodles or cavatappi

If using a whole chicken, cover completely with water in a large pot and boil slowly until completely cooked. When done, remove from pot to cool and add all ingredients except for corn and lima beans. Debone the chicken and return the meat to the pot, tearing it into manageable chunks. Add lima beans and corn and cook slowly for 2-3 hours.

If using chicken breasts, dice and set to boiling in a pot with at least two quarts of water, then add the other ingredients when the chicken is completely cooked.

In the last half-hour of cooking, you can either boil noodles separately or just add to the pot (you may need to add some boiling water to ensure the noodles are covered).

I've always thought this was more a soup than stew, as it makes a broth, rather than gravy. Given the kids' aversion to lima beans, I have substituted green beans on more than one occasion. Play around with the spices as you like (I've made this one with curry powder before!).

Chili!

The exclamation mark is no mistake; a good chili is a great asset to have at one's disposal. Many freakishly cold, snow-packed days in the North have been punctuated with a warm, thick chili. There are as many ways to make chili as there are people who eat it. Some like it hot, some like it mild, some like it thick, and others like it soupy. However you prefer it, don't forget to add some cheese on top. . .

1 Tbsp. olive oil
1.5 Lbs. ground beef or chuck (you can also use steak or roast)
1 Large onion, chopped
1 Green bell pepper, chopped
2 Jalapeño peppers, seeded and chopped
1 Can diced tomatoes and chilies
1 Can tomato sauce
1 Can light red kidney beans
1 Tbsp. chili powder
1 Tsp. crushed red pepper
Shredded cheese (sharp cheddar or Monterey Jack)

In a three-quart saucepan, heat oil and sauté onions and jalapeños until the onions become slightly translucent and the peppers become fragrant. Remove from pot and set aside. In the same pan, brown beef and drain off any grease. Combine all ingredients except the cheese, stirring well to break up the tomatoes. Simmer over medium-low heat for about thirty minutes, stirring occasionally. If desired, this can be turned into a chili-mac with the addition of 7-10 oz. of prepared elbow macaroni. Sprinkle generously with cheese when serving. If this mixture is too thick, adding water or more tomato sauce will thin things out a bit.

Onion Soup

Onions have a very high concentration of flavonoids and phenolics, which have antioxidant and even *anticancer* properties. They help manage cholesterol, and jazz up the flavor of almost any dish, so why not make them a dish of their own? Onion soup can be found on the appetizer menu of just about any restaurant worth visiting, and is an easy task to master for the dedicated adventurer.

8 Cups sliced yellow onions (approximately 2.5 lbs.)
6 Tbsp. butter
4 Tsp. granulated sugar
2 Quarts reduced-sodium chicken broth
½ Cup brandy
Salt and pepper to taste
8 Slices French bread, toasted
Grated Romano cheese

Cook onions in butter in a large saucepan until they are tender, stirring often. Sprinkle sugar over onions and cook, stirring, another minute. Add broth; cover and bring to boil. Reduce heat and simmer for 15 minutes to blend flavors. Add brandy and cook for another two minutes. Serve in oven-safe bowls. Float toast on top and lavishly sprinkle with cheese. Broil just long enough for cheese to melt and then brown slightly.

Beef Stew

Another stovetop and campfire basic, beef stew is a hearty fare that is easily prepared and always well-met at any gathering, especially on cold, winter days. Nothing quite rounds out a day like coming in from chopping wood, snowshoeing, etc. like walking into the house and smelling that thick aroma wafting through the air.

1 Can beef broth
1 Round steak cut into 1 inch pieces
3 Cups diced potatoes
1 Bag baby carrots
1 Can of peas
3-5 Cloves garlic, minced
1 Yellow onion coarsely chopped
½ Cup Cabernet
Salt, pepper, cayenne, thyme, basil to taste **
2 Tbsp. cornstarch
Olive oil
Worcestershire Sauce

Brown steak slowly, drizzling with Worcestershire sauce. Reserve drippings and place meat in a large pot with potatoes, carrots, and onions. Bronze garlic in olive oil and add to pot. Pour in wine and broth and add water as needed to cover potatoes, and then bring to boil until potatoes are done. Reduce heat and simmer, adding spices to taste. Add cornstarch to reserved beef drippings (if the drippings do not make up at least a cup, add water). Stir well to dissolve cornstarch and add to pot. Pour in peas and simmer for 15-20 minutes. Serve with biscuits.

**I use 1 tsp. thyme, 1 tsp. basil, ½ tsp. pepper, ½ tsp. cayenne, and ¼ tsp. salt

What about the Bread?

I have seen people make such a fuss over the type of bread they serve for specific meals, wondering to myself, "What does it matter". Early on, I can recall that it never did. Our family served biscuits with soups and stews just as quickly as slices of sandwich bread. The only rule to adhere to is *"Don't forget the bread"*! The true adventurer always keeps biscuits at the ready, whether store-bought, ready-to-cook dough or the pack-in mixture mentioned back in Chapter I. Now, some people do try to get fancy with their beef stew and stick it in a casserole dish with a crust of biscuit dough on top, with the intention to bake it like a big shepherd's pie. *If you want to make a shepherd's pie, mash up some potatoes and make a shepherd's pie.* Baking biscuits on the top of stew rarely comes out well, with the results being either half-raw dough, or biscuits so soggy from drawing the stew juices into them that they just fall apart. There are very few culinary failures as unappetizing as 'Beef Stew with Goo'.

Left: Biscuits rising by the wood stove. Right: The finished product, right from the oven.

CHAPTER IV

Fast Times, Slow Cookers...

The slow cooker is your little friend in the kitchen that says, "I know you have a lot to do, so let me take care of dinner". Basically, all you have to do is dump a bunch of stuff into your slow-cooker, set it for the proper temperature and, barring power outages or other accidents, set about your day knowing that dinner will be ready when you arrive. Including those listed above, there are many soup and stew recipes that can be made in the slow cooker, plus any number of slow-roast dishes from roast beef and vegetables to stuffed peppers. Many slow cookers are quite easy to transport, thus allowing you to bring a dish along with you when meeting friends. Even though electricity is available in most campgrounds nowadays, it is generally best to remember that slow cookers are an *indoor* tool, as the smell of slow-roasted foods wafting through the woods from atop your picnic table may likely attract visitors of the fuzzy *and not always tiny* variety.

Slow cookers come in many forms, from electric pots to countertop roasters. They are usually always electrically powered, though a stew pot or cauldron over a well-tended, controlled fire would also serve well. The idea, though, is that you set it about its business so you can go about yours. Slow cookers *do* require a little advanced planning, as you would usually start it cooking sometime in the morning, before heading out on the day's adventures.

I have experimented with a large number of protein/vegetable combinations, leading to an arsenal of meal ideas that we strive to keep ingredients "at the ready" for. We always have chili fixin's in stock, and usually give some thought come grocery time for what we may be wanting to slow-roast next. Prep time varies from "dump it all in and turn the pot on" to "we're making dinner sometime between breakfast and lunch". Most of the soups and stews I mentioned before belong to the former group, although the proteins need to be seared beforehand to keep them from drying out as they cook. Also, it gives a great boost to visual presentation, as beef will, depending on the moisture present during cooking, sometimes turn *grey* if it's just thrown into the pot raw. There are few things more unappealing than a boiled roast.

On that note, it should be understood that slow cookers are *closed* cookers. Even if there is a vent in the lid, there is very little evaporation going on during the cooking process. You can actually *dry out* your proteins by adding too much liquid. You should also limit the amount of broth or other juices in stew recipes, as they will come out like soups. It takes a bit of practice, but at least you can eat your mistakes.

What follows are some additional recipes that can be easily adapted to the slow cooker, stovetop, or oven. Some of these recipes do not specify the amount of meat involved. The average serving size for beef is around 4-6 ounces (cooked weight). You should aim for about 6-8 uncooked ounces per adult. A note on safety—if you want to mix everything together the night before to keep in the fridge until morning, DO NOT include the meat. Always keep your proteins, especially poultry, separate from all other ingredients until you are ready to start them cooking! With that said, it's time to get started. Remember to experiment as you go. . .

Teriyaki Beef

This one is as simple as it sounds, but works well for plated meals and sandwiches, alike. I've used small steaks, roasts cut into strips, and even stew meat for this recipe. The flavors involved lend themselves especially well to grilled vegetables or an accompanying baked potato (see "Homesteader Potato", pg. 65)

Bob Wilkins

Steak or roast, cut into strips
Teriyaki sauce
One medium onion, chopped
One bell pepper, chopped
4 oz. chopped mushrooms
Any good barbeque sauce

Place meat in a bowl and add ¼ cup teriyaki sauce. Let stand for 15-30 minutes.

Heat 1 Tbsp. olive oil over medium heat and sauté onions, mushrooms, and pepper until the onions just become tender. Set aside.

Brown the meat, peppering it generously, until seared on all sides.

Place seared meat in cooker.

Mix about ¼ cup of barbeque sauce with the teriyaki sauce and pour over meat. Cover with the sautéed veg.

Cook on high for 1 hour, then low for 5.

Chicken Corn Chowder

3 Cups milk
1 Lb. chicken breast, cubed
1 Cup diced onions
2 Cups diced potatoes (OR shred them into hash browns)
2 Cans cream-style corn
1 Can cream of mushroom soup
1 Small can OR ½ cup fresh, chopped mushrooms
1 Tbsp. dried parsley
1 Bag (16 oz.) frozen corn
Salt, Pepper, and Cayenne to taste

Dump everything but the chicken into the slow cooker and stir everything up well (it helps to break the frozen corn up in the bag before you pour it in).

Add the chicken to the mixture, pushing them to the bottom to ensure they cook thoroughly.

Cook on low for about 8 hours or high for 5.

This makes a pretty healthy batch, but any leftovers keep well in the fridge, or can be frozen.

Jamaican Pork Stew

1 Tbsp. Olive oil
1 ½ lbs. boneless pork chops, cubed
2 Tsp. flour
2 Medium onions, thinly sliced
2 Cloves garlic, crushed
4 Tsp. rum (light or dark)
2 (16 oz.) cans tomatoes, drained and crushed
¼ Tsp crushed red pepper flakes
1 Tsp fresh-ground black pepper
¼ Tsp ground allspice
2 Cups beef broth
4 Small potatoes, diced
2 Tsp. dark molasses
Salt to taste
Cooked rice

Begin by heating the oil in a good-sized pan. Dust pork with flour and brown in oil, a few pieces at a time. Remove with a slotted spoon and place in slow cooker.

Sauté onion until it just begins to get tender, and then add in garlic, constantly stirring until it becomes fragrant. Add rum and scrape up any browned bits from the pan, then dump it all (onions, garlic, pan leavings, rum) over the pork in the slow cooker.

Add all remaining ingredients, stirring well, then cook on low for about 8 hours. Serve over rice.

Stout Stew

2 Lbs. stew beef
3 Tbsp. oil
3 Tbsp. flour
½ Tsp. salt
½ Tsp. pepper

Cayenne to taste
2 Large onions
1 Garlic clove, crushed
2 Tbsp. tomato paste dissolved in 4 Tbsp. water
1¼ Cup stout**
2 Cups diced carrots
3 Cups cubed potatoes
2 Cups diced celery
1 Tsp. thyme

Trim meat into two inch cubes and coat with 1 Tbsp. oil. Season flour with salt, pepper, and cayenne, and then coat the meat (it helps to do this in a big zippered storage bag).

Heat the remaining oil in a large skillet and sear the meat on all sides. Reduce the heat and add the onions, garlic, and tomato paste to the skillet and cook gently for about five minutes.

Pour the skillet's contents into the slow cooker.

Pour just under half of the stout into the pan and bring it to a boil, stirring to dissolve the meat leavings in the pan. Pour this over the meat in the slow cooker, and then add the remaining stout.

Add veg and thyme, and then stir well.

Cook on low for about 3 hours.

A friend of mine has tried this using a dark cola as substitute for the Stout. This is a good way to go if you neither have nor want to use an alcoholic beverage!

Beef Burgundy

6 Slices of bacon
2 Lbs. stew beef
¼ Cup flour
1 ½ Cups burgundy
¾ Cup beef broth
8 Oz. mini carrots
3 Tbsp. chopped parsley

1 Bay leaf
3 Cloves garlic, minced
¾ Tsp. salt
½ Tsp. dried thyme
¼ Tsp. pepper
8 Oz. mushrooms, sliced

In a deep pan, cook bacon until it is crisp, then drain on paper towels. Chop coarsely and set aside.

In the bacon drippings, cook beef until browned, then set aside.

Sprinkle flour over the leavings in the pan, and cook, stirring constantly, until completely combined.

Slowly stir in wine and broth. Bring the mixture to a boil; reduce heat and cook, stirring occasionally, until it thickens a bit.

Place beef and all other ingredients in slow cooker and then pour in the wine/broth mixture. Stir well.

Cook on low for six hours. You can rush this to about 4 hours on high, but your carrots might still be a bit crunchy.

A Nod to Casseroles—

Casseroles are, for all intents and purposes, foods of convenience. Casseroles come in two forms: Those you intended to make and those that just happen. There is little to distinguish the former from recipes we have already seen. The latter, however, is basically the home chef's fridge cleaner. If you have pasta and cream of anything soup, you can turn most of the contents of your refrigerator into something that bystanders will think you actually meant to happen. One of the simplest casseroles my family was ever responsible for (and voluntarily claimed its creation) combined a box of macaroni and cheese, a can of tuna, a can of peas, and the aforementioned cream of mushroom soup (with a little help from some Cajun spices). It was simple, it took a single pan to make, and the kids could do it easily, if the mood hit. We called it, simply, *Tuna Noodle Glop*, and it was perfect for those times when we were feeling ridiculously lazy.

But enough about the indoors. . . Let's go outside. . .

CHAPTER V

Foods that Go. . .

Once, while backpacking with a friend, we found ourselves in a rainy situation that was not conducive to building a fire. Being the middle of July in Appalachia, we were warm enough, once we pitched the tent and changed into dry clothes, but we didn't have the ability to heat up water for our MRE packets. In this situation, any backpacker worth their salt always has a standby, and my friend (who was in charge of provisions) was no exception. Our choices were trail mix and little jars of baby food. Needless to say, it wasn't long before I used a foil emergency blanket to fashion a small awning and set about building a cook fire. One bite of strained squash was enough for me to entertain notions of cannibalism.

In the noble spirit of adventuring, sometimes we are required to 'carry in'. Be it a bike trek, hiking trip, or just taking the family sightseeing, it isn't always practical to take time to cook, let alone haul in what you would need to accomplish the task. Thanks to modern technology, there is an abundance of choices at hand, from thermoses for hot soups and beverages, to soft-shell coolers for packing both warm and cold items. What you carry just depends on the amount of prep time you want to spend and the amount of care you are willing to take on the journey. There are any number of energy bars and portable foods available from stores, so here are just a few ideas before you go racing down the trail. . .

Sandwiches

"Really?" you're thinking to yourself. "After all the fuss he's gone through writing this book, he is really going to waste time talking about sandwiches?"

Short answer: yes.

Sandwiches are elegant in their simplicity and can be easily packed, as long as you remember a few simple rules like, 'don't use mayonnaise on hundred-degree days', and such. Simple PBJs are filling and will pack for a long time with little care. Lunchmeats will require a small cooler, but are still pretty easy to work with. It helps, if you are going to pack your sandwiches with leafy greens and tomatoes, to use 'tuck and fold' style sandwich bags, as the zip-to-seal variety will cause your bread to become soggy after a while.

Cold meals are fine for traveling during the warmer months of the year, but adventurers often find themselves out in the wild long after the winds have cooled and the leaves have fallen. In these instances, a little warmth is comforting on the long trail. "Carry in" foods that retain their warmth well are rare, yes, but a few gems do exist. One of those is the Cornish pasty. . .

Cornish Pasties

No, not 'pastry', *pasty*! A meal for royalty and commoners alike, the pasty was carried to all parts of the world by immigrant Cornish miners. Originally made with venison, pasties have taken several forms over the years, including 'two-course' pasties, which included a dessert such as baked apples on one side, with the meat and veg on the other. However it is made, it is a complete meal in a crust, dense enough to hold its heat for hours, if properly wrapped. I've kept pasties warm for exceptionally long periods of time wrapped in foil and socked away in a small cooler. They do require quite a bit of prep time, but are well worth it, especially if a good, hot meal would be welcome on your journey. The following recipe makes 6 medium-sized pasties. They can be eaten by hand or with a fork, and are excellent with a little ketchup. Some places actually serve them with gravy, but pasty purists will wrinkle their nose at the thought.

¾ Pound lean ground beef
2 Cups diced, peeled potatoes
1 Cup diced, peeled rutabaga
½ Cup chopped onion
½ Tsp. salt
2½ Cups all-purpose flour
½ Cup vegetable shortening
⅓-½ Cup water
1 Large egg

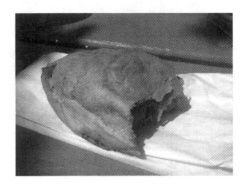

Preheat oven to 400°. Combine beef, potatoes, rutabaga, onion, and salt in a medium bowl. Mix well and set aside.

Place flour in a large bowl. Cut in shortening with a pastry blender until coarse crumbs form. Combine ⅓ cup water and egg in a small bowl; beat well. Add egg mixture to flour mixture. Toss with a fork until the mixture sticks together, adding more water (a little at a time) until a soft dough forms.

Place dough on a lightly floured surface and divide into 6 equal pieces. Roll each piece out to form an 8-inch round.

Spoon ½ cup of the beef mixture onto one half of each round. Brush the edges of dough with water and then fold dough over to form a half-moon. Press edges to seal; place on baking sheet. Cut several slits in top of each for steam to escape.

Bake pasties until crust is golden, about 40-50 minutes. Remove from baking sheet and place on a wire rack to cool slightly before serving or wrapping.

***An excellent shortcut is to pick up some refrigerated pie dough. They're already in formed rounds and this cuts your overall prep time in half!**

Energy Bars

Sounds simple enough, right? Just whip by the supermarket, pick up a box of energy bars, fill the canteen, and hit the trail. Maybe so, but it helps when you grab a box to read the label. There is a litany of choices and not all of them are truly balanced in the nutrition they provide. What should you be looking for?

- **Carbohydrates** are your body's main fuel source. Carbohydrates are nutrients that break down into glucose. All carbs are not the same, however. Both naturally occurring sugars and sugars added to foods are broken down quickly, but if they are not bundled with other nutrients, they are basically empty calories. Quality carbs are found in whole grains and low fat dairy. These take longer to digest and will provide more steady energy; a must if you are looking at a day of strenuous cycling or hiking. The common rule of thumb for the average human adult is that carbohydrates should make up between 40-60% of the daily nutritional intake.

- **Protein** is the material your body uses to build and maintain muscle, bone, skin, and hair. Protein is a secondary energy source. If your body is lacking in carbohydrates, it will chemically break down the protein in the musculature until those proteins behave like carbohydrates. This process will cause muscle loss and is hard on the liver and kidneys, as both are working double-time to filter out the unused by-products. High protein bars provide adequate energy for activity that is not so intense, but are best for recovery snacks *after* strenuous workouts (again, assuming they are balanced with quality carbohydrates). In general, adults require between 60 to 80 grams of protein daily.

- **Calories** are a unit of measurement of the energy a food provides. The body has no idea, however, where these calories come from, whether it be carbohydrates, proteins, fats, alcohol, etc. The simple fact is that you will gain weight if you take in more calories than you burn off in your activities. This being the case, you must pay attention to the *quality* of calories you ingest. *Empty calories* are calories with no nutritional value, such as from solid fats and sugars. Consuming a large amount of sugar may give you a rush of energy, but it will wear off long before you've burned off the calories that came with it. A good rule of thumb: Aim for quality ingredients and pay attention to your protein/carb levels.

- **Caffeine** is a metabolic stimulant that directly affects the central nervous system. It is used in countless foods and beverages all over the world to reduce fatigue and improve clarity and focus. In some products, it is given in massive doses to both boost energy and promote fat loss through speeding up the metabolism. There seem to be as many detriments as there are benefits to using caffeine, but the simple fact is that it will not be vanishing from the world market any time soon. One should simply be cautious with caffeine levels in their energy snacks. Obviously, if you are going to be hiking the wilderness, a case of the jitters isn't as big an issue as if you were, say, rock climbing.

Keeping all of this in mind, there are many excellent choices you could take along with you, usually of the granola variety, which provide long, slow energy burn without weighing your system down with heavy proteins or other nonsense, and also keeping your pack light for the hike back.

Another alternative, of course, is to make your own:

Apricot Bars

. . . Or cherry, or cranberry, etc. I've found that these bars can be made with a variety of dried fruits, and can be easily packed anywhere with little fuss. In a food processor, chop:

1 Cup dried apricots
¾ Cup almonds
¾ Cup walnuts
Then mix fruit and nuts up with:
½ Cup honey
½ Cup wheat germ
⅔ Cup flour
2 Tbsp. oil
Add enough liquid (I use apple juice) to form a thick batter, usually 2-4 tbsp.

Preheat oven to 375°. Mix well. Press into an 8x8 inch square greased pan and bake for 30 minutes, or until firm. Cut into 12 bars and leave in the pan to cool. Later, package individually and store in a refrigerator or freezer. Contains approximately 220 calories per bar.

Trail Mix

A friend of mine describes trail mix as "candy with obstacles". Trail mix is a nutritious snack with a salty/sweet balance and a portability factor of 9.5. Before heading on your next adventure, mix:

1 Cup raisins
1 Cup unsalted walnuts
1 Cup roasted unsalted soy nuts (I've used peanuts as well, also unsalted)
1 Cup chocolate chips (you can substitute carob chips for a healthier alternative)
½ Cup chopped dried dates
½ Tsp. sea salt

The bottom line is that trail mix does not have to be boring. Add some crystallized ginger or dried fruit. Some people prefer shredded coconut, but I just don't like picking it out of my teeth as I'm walking a forest trail. Dried blueberries add excellent flavor, as well as apricots and cherries!

Jerky

Until the advent of refrigeration, there were very few methods available to preserve meat. Unless you lived in the far north, where the ambient temperatures would help to preserve your stores, drying, smoking, and pickling were your only options. Large chunks of meat were preserved for home use, but for traveling, things like Jerky and Pemmican were often-used staples. Jerky can be made from just about any meat imaginable, though the most prevalent are beef and venison. Jerky can be cured using a brine solution, by smoking, or by simply drying the meat. Brining involves soaking the meat in a sweet pickle brine (described below), then drying in a cool place. The meat is sliced, and then hung on racks to cold smoke at 75-85° for 12 to 36 hours. The jerky is ready if it snaps when folded. A dehydrator or smoker makes the process much faster and easier, but if you have neither, jerky can also be made in the oven. The process, in a nutshell:

- **Pick your cut of meat**. Lean meats are always best, as the fat harbors bacteria that can cause spoilage during the drying process.
- **Trim the fat**. Slice the meat in narrow strips and remove as much fat as you can.
- **Spice things up**. Marinating is an option, but the additional juices can prolong the drying time. Play with different blends of spices and rubs. Generally, a good steak rub will make for excellent beef jerky.
- **Dehydrating**. Again, this process is simpler if you have a dehydrator. Make certain your jerky strips are far enough apart to allow for airflow all around and follow the guidelines in your dehydrator's manual.
- **If you only have an oven**. . . Preheat the oven to 160°. Place the meat in the oven on a wire rack with a pan beneath to catch any drippings. Let it cook for 1-3 hours, depending on the meat. Check on it after the first 60 minutes and every 30 minutes, thereafter.
- **Storage**. Put it in a cool, dry place. Mason jars are nice, but vacuum-sealed bags are best. Refrigerate or freeze until you're ready to use. Homemade jerky usually keeps for 2-3 weeks.

For brining and smoking:

- 4 Oz. pickling spice
- 2½ Gallons water
- 2 ½ Lbs. salt
- 3 Cloves garlic
- 1 Lb. sugar

Simmer spice in a cup of water for about 10 minutes, then mix with the remaining water and other ingredients. Chill to 35° and add meat.

Pemmican

Pemmican is a "survival superfood", as it is made of pure, dried protein and rendered fats, and will keep for exceptionally long periods without going rancid. It can be spiced, which is probably a good idea, since most people who have tried pemmican have likened it to eating mediocre dog food (I did *not* ask how they knew). It is a high-energy food, first devised by Native Americans, and then later adopted by explorers, traders, and armies, alike. There are abundant accounts of people eating pemmican raw, but it was also cooked into stews, usually made from whatever other ingredients existed where those sometimes hapless adventurers found themselves. Native Americans would chew a piece for as long as it would last; a method most would find surprisingly filling.

The preparation is quite simple:

- Pound jerky into a powder or run it through a grinder or food processor.
- Add nuts, seeds, or finely chopped dried fruit.
- Render beef fat down to liquid, straining out any chunky bits.
- Bind the entire mixture together using the beef fat.
- Roll the pemmican into balls.
- Store in a closed container in a cool, dry location.

Remember that pemmican was used by people *who had no other choice*. There was little chance of resupplying on a journey across the vast wilderness, so groups had to carry *everything* they were going to need. In his writings in 1874, Seargent-Major Sam Steele of the Northwest Mounted Police told of the pemmican stew, called "rubaboo", made by the explorers of the Canadian fur trade. The stew consisted of water, flour, and (if they were lucky enough to find them) potatoes or wild onions. It could also be fried in a pan, either alone or with onions or potatoes. It should be noted that Seargent-Major Steele said that he "never had a taste for it [raw]".

CHAPTER VI

Breakfast!

Even familiar, canned meats make excellent fare, when paired with eggs!

You've all heard it said that 'breakfast is the most important meal of the day'. That first bit of food you stuff in your face sets the tone for your day; it tells your metabolism what it's in for. Nutritionists, health nuts, weight loss fanatics, scientists, librarians, and construction workers will all tell you to grab something in the morning before getting started and, you know what? They're right.

Eggs

Eggs are awesome, little protein bombs (avg. 6 grams of protein, each) that have been on both sides of the nutritional fence over the course of the last several decades. One of the main reasons for this has been *cholesterol*. There is about 187 mg of cholesterol in the average egg. The kicker is, *your body makes its own cholesterol*, and so, even if you don't eat that egg, you will still have it in your system! Here's a fast and loose biology lesson:

- All of the cells in your body have the ability to make cholesterol, as they use it to create protective membranes
- Cholesterol is a building block for Vitamin D, as well as estrogen and testosterone
- If your body doesn't think its cells have enough cholesterol to do their job, it calls up the liver for assistance
- The liver produces ¾ of the body's cholesterol (up to 1000 mg a day!)
- The breakdown of carbohydrates, proteins, and fats from the food you eat releases carbon, which the liver turns into cholesterol.
- The average diet only adds about 300-500 mg of cholesterol to the whole mess

Genetics plays a large part in the overall process, as well. Some people have high cholesterol because their bodies do not recognize that they are ingesting it adequately through their diet, and it does not slow down its own production. So what does this all mean? Essentially, regular checkups with your doctor are a good idea, and the nutritive properties of an egg far outweigh its bad points.

There are so many ways to cook an egg, you could spend an entire day experimenting and still not try them all.

Poaching—

Poaching eggs is fairly easy, with a little bit of practice. A perfect poached egg is, basically, a solid white with a runny yolk. There are several methods to choose from, but the one I like most is the "simmering water" method, as you can perform this little task over a fire or camp stove just as easily as in your home kitchen.

- In a small to medium saucepan, bring some water to a good, steady simmer.
- Add a dash of vinegar to the water.
- Crack your egg into a small cup or bowl (this makes inserting it into the water much easier).
- Stir the water in the pan until you get a steady "whirlpool" motion. This actually helps hold the egg together when you pour it in.
- Pour the egg into the center of the whirlpool, as close to the surface as you can manage.

- Let the egg cook for three minutes. Don't touch it, stir it, poke at it, or even stare at it too intently. It will be done in three minutes.
- Take the egg out of the water with a slotted spoon and drain it for a bit on a paper towel (you don't want eggy water all over the plate, do you?).
- Season to taste

When done properly, a poached egg will be a usually teardrop-shaped pocket with a firm white and runny yolk. Do not get discouraged if this doesn't happen on your first dozen tries. Just remember, if your egg white is still a bit runny, shoot for a slightly longer cooking time. If the yolk is starting to solidify, then aim shorter. The egg pictured here could have used another few seconds, as the white is still glistening. Practice makes perfect!

At this point, I feel the need to admit that I have, in a moment of laziness, tried to poach eggs in the microwave. This method is the most frustrating for me, as your egg can, in fact *explode*. Basically, you just crack an egg into a small, microwaveable bowl of water (about a half-cup) and cover it with a plate. Nuke it on high for a minute. If, after a minute, it still isn't quite right, cook it no more than 15 seconds at a time until it's done. Some people swear by this method, but I've never been able to get it just right (though I *have* scared the tar out of a couple family pets).

Scrambling

Scrambling is, by far, the easiest way to cook an egg in a pan. Basically, you just crack your eggs into a bowl or measuring cup, beat them to within an inch of their lives, and start cooking. The more vigorously you beat the eggs, the fluffier they will be.

- Beat eggs, adding anything you think would go good in them. Basic salt and pepper, or add sliced mushrooms and onions, cheese, or even salsa!

- Heat about two tablespoons of butter in a nonstick pan over medium heat (you can use cooking spray if butter gives you the willies).
- Pour in the eggs, slowly folding them as they solidify. The best way to do this is with your flipper *inverted*. Rather than trying to flip the eggs, you actually *pull* them across the pan. This is what gives scrambled eggs that fluffy, curd-shape. Keep folding the eggs until they are completely cooked.
- Serve immediately! Scrambled eggs will cool off quickly. And no cheating, leaving them in the pan. The heat of the pan will continue to cook them, and no one likes overcooked eggs.

A fun little note is that most people tend to avoid cooking eggs in cast iron pans, as the eggs harmlessly take on a greenish color. I wonder if that may have been the inspiration for something?

Boiled

"Really," you're thinking. "He really thinks we need to be told how to boil an egg?" The short answer is "yes". Now be patient and I'll tell you what you've been doing wrong all these years. It won't take long.

Basically, the best way to boil an egg is to *not* boil it at all. Cover your eggs about an inch deep in a pan with *cold* water, and then bring it to a good simmer over medium heat. A hard-cooked egg usually takes right at eight minutes to be perfect. Keep in mind, you don't start timing until *after* the water comes to a good simmer, and you may have to adjust the heat during the eight minutes to keep the water from coming to a boil. Drain the eggs and run cold water over them to cool them off. A perfect hard-cooked egg will have a solid, just about crumbly yolk, and there will be no greyish-green ring around the yolk (a sign of overcooking).

You're welcome.

Frying

Basically, I'm going to stop right here. I dislike frying eggs for anyone other than myself or the kids, because EVERYONE has a different preference. "Over Easy" can mean several different things for as many people, as well as "Sunnyside", "Eggs in a Basket", etc. The one thing I can offer is that breakfast doesn't have to be devoid of vegetables. A method I've become enamored with, of late, is actually using vegetable rings as handy, in-pan egg cookers.

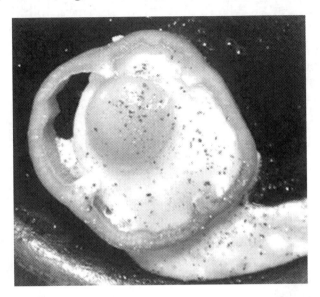

Though sometimes the egg escapes if the pan isn't hot enough, having a little leakage is preferable to burning the underside of the egg. Once the egg begins to set up well, it can be flipped easily, as the vegetable ring will help hold it in place. Pictured here is an egg in a bell pepper, but eggs are great in onion rings, as well!

At this point, I think it's plain that we could go on and on about eggs, in general. Eggs are *wonderful*, yes, but not the only thing to be served up at breakfast time. I suppose, what I'm getting at is, what about. . .

Meat!

Protein! Well, *more* protein, anyway. This is the point at which you can really be creative. Whether you are popping open a can of corned beef hash, frying up sausage or bacon, laying down a hearty steak, or just frying up a mess of bologna, just about anything will round out the plate nicely. Most of these proteins are easily cooked. As long as you don't blacken them, you're fine. Sausage needs to be cooked slowly, as you don't want any raw bits lurking in the center of the patties or links. Bacon can cause a ruckus, as it is very easy to turn it into a substance that becomes crumbly powder when bitten.

Bacon

The best way to cook bacon is actually with *water*, rather than in just its own fat. I was shown this method on a camping trip in Eastern Kentucky. A few backpackers had wandered into the campground in which we were nested and decided to cook up a mess of bacon on their first morning there. The bacon was purchased from the smallish camp store, but they carried everything else in. Having nothing but a mess kit, the group's elected chef for the morning covered his bacon in water and proceeded to school me in something I thought I was already thoroughly versed in. Here's how it went:

- Place the bacon strips in your pan and add just enough water to cover them
- Over a relatively high heat, bring the water to the boiling point, and then adjust your temperature/position over the fire to keep the water simmering.
- Once the water has simmered away, lower the heat yet again, in order to brown the bacon to its desired crispiness.

This method keeps the bacon from shriveling up and, actually, will cause it to plump, as the water helps the meat retain its natural juices. Who knew?

Sausage

Sausage is quite simple, if you take care. Preheat your skillet for a bit over a medium heat, and then cook the sausage patties for about 12-14 minutes, flipping them frequently to prevent scorching. The aim is an internal temperature of about 160°F (make sure the juices run clear).

Did I Mention Potatoes?

Breakfast potatoes are simple and should not be overthought. Most varieties are fried, whether shredded or sliced. Care should be taken to not use too much oil, as it is next to impossible to drain off. Season with salt and pepper, or get creative with a garlic and herb blend. I use about 3-4 tablespoons of butter, enough potatoes for the group (cut into smallish chunks, sometimes with the skin on), and seasoned pepper to taste with a little garlic powder. I cook them over medium heat until they start to brown on all sides, as I can't stand raw potatoes.

Moving On. . .

If you haven't guessed by now from the overall theme of this book, the main idea here is *creativity*. Taking simple ingredients and making them stand out is the hallmark of adventurous cooking. Your situation will dictate what you use (sliced summer sausage or bologna is easier to cook up than more involved meats when you're away from the kitchen), and experience gained from practice will tell you what you should bring with you.

The observant adventurer probably thought several pages back, "Hey! Isn't this out of order, somewhat?" Yes, I did extensively cover a litany of dinner recipes and methods before we got to breakfast. The reason behind this is that, mostly, breakfast ends up being the *second* meal you prepare when going out into the wilderness or starting out on that weekend trip after the kids get home from school on Friday afternoon. The key to proper advance planning is not just knowing what you are going to be doing, but the order in which you will be doing it. Up to this point (aside from a few notes otherwise), most of our cooking has been centered on the home, whether in the kitchen or out in the yard. Let's head farther out, now, and take a look at what it takes to truly cook in the wild. . .

Chapter VII

To Camp!

So, you have it in your head that you want to get back to nature. Setting out for the deep woods with a group of friends or family isn't such a daunting task, with a little planning. An impromptu camping excursion, however, can be likened unto survival camping in a great many ways. The order is always the same: Fire, shelter, food & water. Depending on how fast the trip was thrown together, you could be fully equipped, or you could end up trying to feed your crew with nothing more than a few cans of beans and, "Holy cats, do we NOT have a can opener?!!"

I have some basic requirements on my list when I set out camping, depending mostly upon how many are going to be in the group. If there are just a couple, each person carries in a mess kit, hopefully with one smallish stew pot. If the group consists of quite a few (myself, Kim, and all four kids, for example), you are going to want to carry in some substantially more capable equipment.

When camping with the family, I make certain we have at least one sauté pan, a good-sized stew pot, and enough plates and bowls for everyone. All of our cookware is capable of going right over the fire, and we have a grate that we take with us that makes campfire cooking that much easier. A tea kettle for heating water quickly is a good idea, plus a basin to wash dishes after the meal. Eating utensils take many forms, from the basic hobo tool, which includes a knife, can/bottle opener, and a fork and spoon attachment, to backpacking 'sporks' (shown below), and even inexpensive flatware. Whichever you decide to bring, any will make your trip immeasurably more enjoyable.

A simple backpacker's "spork" is a handy tool to have, doesn't take up much room, and is fairly inexpensive. This spork is made of BPA-free, heat-resistant material, has a small, serrated cutting edge, and can be picked up at any sporting goods store for around $3.00.

You can plan your camping trip right down to how you will be cooking your fresh-caught fish over an open fire but, ultimately, you will find yourself supping on beans and Vienna sausages (assuming you remembered to bring them). The first rule of camp cooking is to **never assume that you will be able to catch/find/purchase food at your destination**. If you are planning to catch fish, go fishing! If you are planning to catch game (that is in season), by all means, go hunting! The main thing is to make like a Boy Scout and **always be prepared**! Remember what I said about the hiking trip and the baby food? Nature is a chaotic system; you can count on any number of things to screw up your plans. Trust me, getting caught in a multi-day downpour in a boreal forest is much easier to deal with if you thought to bring along MREs and a small cook stove!

Cooking with Fire

Even though we carry a propane stove on camping excursions, most of our cooking is done over an open fire. This does, indeed, take a knack. There are many things to consider before starting a fire, the primary concern being, "could

I start a much larger fire by accident?" Spending time in nature requires one to be aware of their surroundings. This includes clearing the area of anything that could cause the fire to spread out of your control. Even in a campground, where fire rings are usually provided, a carelessly-tended fire could potentially ignite a much larger blaze. Things to look for before even constructing your fire lay are:

- Dry leaves or needles
- Dry grasses
- Low-hanging trees, especially evergreens
- Steady or gusting winds
- Garbage or other human detritus

The last one is bigger than you may think. Once, while getting a fire together in a campground fire pit for a college party, we found ourselves dodging flying fireworks that had been left buried in the ashes of a previous fire! Who throws spent fireworks into a campfire?!!!

The actual lay of the fire is going to be determined by what you want to do with it. Obviously, if your goal is to jam a stick through a hot dog and roast it on the fire, you don't need to give much thought to the arrangement of the fire lay; a tipi fire will work just fine. If you are planning to cook with pots and pans, a little forethought is required. We will get into other types of fire lays in the 'Survival' chapter. For camp cooking, I use two basic fire lays:

Hunter's Fire Lay—One of the most useful fire lays for cooking with pots and pans, the Hunter's Lay involves building the fire between two large logs of similar size. The logs give you a stable place upon which to rest a pot, pan, or teakettle, while leaving a channel through which fuel can be added. The channel allows the air flow to be controlled inasmuch as you can position the logs perpendicular to the breeze on windy days. Arrange your tinder in the center between the two logs and loosely pile small twigs upon that, gradually increasing their size. For a cook fire, you will want to burn some small sticks at first, to build your bed of coals, but as you are cooking, you will feed the fire with larger material, usually about the size of your thumb or a bit bigger. If you need more heat on one side, simply add more fuel. If you need less heat, let that part starve a bit.

Three-Point Fire Lay—When large logs are not available, a three-point lay is very handy. Using three similar-sized rocks or, in the case of the illustration, three tent stakes, you create a surface upon which to place a pot or pan. The drawback is, obviously, that you may only use one pot at a time, as this is going to be a much smaller fire. A simple teepee fire in the middle of the rocks/stakes will suffice. I did learn the hard way that, if you are using tent stakes, you should make certain the ground is solid enough to hold them steady. If you can just push them into the ground with your hand, the chances are they will not long support a full pot of soup, leading to a big mess and a cold dinner of Vienna sausages.

Another method for campfire cooking is to use a grill. In some of the pictures that follow, we used a camp grill (available at most sporting goods stores). These grills are simply constructed, having four foldable legs and a varied cook surface. Their size prevents them from being used by backpackers, but for group campouts, they make life in your outdoor kitchen much easier.

How hot is it?

One of the most challenging facets of campfire cookery is gauging and controlling temperature. The simplest method is the 'Hand Thermometer'. Basically, hold your hand where the food will go. Count "One-thousand-one, one-thousand-two," etc., for as long as you can stand to hold your hand in that position. Move your hand around to find the temperature you want.

Removed at Count	Heat	Temperature
6 to 8	Slow	250°-350°F
4 to 5	Moderate	350°-400°F
2 to 3	Hot	400°-450°F
1 or less	Very Hot	450°-500°F

I have fire. Now what?

The possibilities are endless! Once you have your fire going, with a stable cooking surface, preparing food isn't much different out here than in the kitchen. Whether you keep it simple with canned meats and soups, or you experiment with grilled fish and stews, *if you've done it on your stovetop, you can do it at camp!*

Breakfast!

Here we are again, at that most important meal of the day! You have been fasting all night, so your body needs adequate nutrition for the day ahead. Cold cereal and breakfast bars may be quick and simple, but a good, hot meal (especially on a cool morning) really wakes everyone up. Skillet toast, ham, and eggs are easy to pack and prepare. A little hot chocolate doesn't hurt, either!

I usually prepare breakfast over the propane stove, though we keep the fire going whenever we are at camp. A mess kit over the fire is fine when it's just you and a friend, but cooking eggs for the family is much easier with a Teflon pan. While everyone is eating, you can be heating your wash water over the campfire and keeping that kettle going for any cocoa refills.

Skillet toast is another item that is ridiculously simple to prepare, yet everyone will make a big deal over. A friend of mine went with me into the Daniel Boone National Forest several years ago on what, I'm sure, was her first camping adventure. Though there was hiking, sightseeing, and all manner of adventure to be had, I am quite certain the highlight of her day was the skillet toast I made with our steak and eggs (she ate nearly half a loaf of bread in the process). All you have to do is butter both sides of a slice of bread and cook it in a pan until it starts to brown on one side, then flip it to brown the other. It's toast, nothing more; but *people will love you for it*!

Lunch!

Okay, we're not going to waste too much time here, as lunch should be the simplest meal of the day. The rules are easy: On a hot day, eat cold; on a cold day, eat hot. Sandwiches are the easiest and quickest way to refuel and get back to the day's activities. Lunchmeat and cheese keeps well in the cooler and sometimes you may get lucky and have some wild edibles about for garnish or dessert. **One should, however, always remember that randomly gnawing on wild plants and berries can be dangerous if you do not know how to properly identify them. Also, if you can't tell a toadstool from a matsutake, *leave mushrooms alone*!!**

A quick, hot lunch could be a hot dog roasted over the fire or a hamburger fried in your mess kit. Soups are excellent morale boosters on days that are cold, rainy, or both. A can of condensed soup can be prepared in very little time with minimal effort, and grilled cheese is never complicated. Maybe you're expecting to have lunch on the trail? Pack in sandwiches or trail mix and jerky. Just remember, the lighter the lunch, the more ravenous your group will be, come dinner time!

Dinner!

This is the adventurer's time to shine! Dinner time is the meal around which the entire group gathers to relive the events of the day and tell stories of their own exploits. Everyone sits about the warm glow of the fire, the heady smell of wood smoke mixed with the aromas of the meal wafting about them. Maybe you were lucky enough to cook up a mess of freshly-caught fish, or everyone gets to tuck into a bowl of campfire soup and biscuits; whichever the case, dinner around the campfire is where memories are truly made.

If You're Going to Grill It, Mean It!

Autumn grilling in Fort Wilkins State Park, Michigan

Grilling is the epitome of outdoor cooking. Whether it's at a roadside park, tailgating at the game, your backyard, or over the fire at your campsite, the unmistakable hiss of juices dripping into the fire combined with the aroma of the smoke and anticipation from everyone around veritably scream, "Great Outdoors"! Grilling is not all about meat and beans, either! With a little finesse, vegetables can be flame-seared or roasted on the grill, also. If there's one thing the Boy Scouts taught me, it's that aluminum foil can be exceptionally handy. Cook onion and pepper slices directly on the grill with partially-shucked ears of corn. Smaller veg and mushrooms can be grilled in specially-made baskets, or just roast it all in a pocket of aluminum foil with a little butter and a vent or two poked in the top. Whichever method you choose, care should be taken, as the vegetables will burn quickly if your fire is too hot.

Campfire Soup

3 Tbsp. butter
2 Large onions, chopped
1 Lb. bag of baby carrots, chopped
2 Celery ribs, sliced
2 13 ½ oz. cans of tomatoes OR 2 14 ½ oz. cans of diced tomatoes
1 10 oz. can diced tomatoes and chilies
2 Cups chicken stock
2 Tbsp. chopped basil
¼ Cup white wine (optional, though recommended)
1 Tsp. sugar
1.5 lbs. stew meat

Melt 2 Tbsp. butter in a large pot over moderate heat. Brown the meat, seasoning with salt and pepper to taste. Remove from pot and set aside.

Melt remaining butter in pot, and then add onions, carrots, and celery, stirring constantly for 2 minutes.

Add wine and cook for another minute. Stir in the tomatoes (if you used whole canned tomatoes, mash them with the end of a wooden spoon).

Add stew meat, sugar, and stock, plus enough water to cover everything. Add basil and give it a good stir.

Let simmer until beef is cooked. As it sits, this recipe serves 4, but can be tweaked to feed a much larger group!

We made this for the first time several years ago, while camping with the kids at a state park on the Lake Michigan shoreline. It was more of an experiment than anything else, as I had never made soup over the campfire before. I felt we needed something warming, as even summer rains in Michigan can be quite chilling. This particular day, a true gully-washer blew in off the lake and the rain fell in sheets. I had just staked down a tarp over the picnic table seconds before the rain hit, and was standing under the van's liftgate, perfectly dry. We decided that the campsite was well-protected enough that we could take a ride to the beach and watch the rest of the storm blow in. It was the exact moment I closed the liftgate that I realized just how much water the little area where your license plate is mounted can hold when it's facing skyward. You never appreciate dry clothes and hot food quite as much as when you are drenched to your boxer shorts in ice water.

Grilling Fish

Grilling any type of seafood may seem daunting at first, but once you have the basics down, it comes fairly easily! A little practice in gauging temperature and time makes all the difference between a nicely-cooked salmon fillet and unintentional sushi. The first thing you need to realize is that any leftover debris, no matter how tiny, is going to stick to your fish. You should clean the grill like crazy, taking time to warm it up so the old stuff breaks loose easier with a wire brush, then coat it with some oil and scrub it again with some soap and water. Before placing the grill over the fire again, you should wipe the grill with an oil-soaked paper towel and brush the fish with an oil or marinade. Make certain the grill is hot before you place the fish on it, because that instant sear helps keep the skin from sticking. Also, placing the fish *across* the grill bars minimizes the amount of contact.

Now, the *type* of fish is just as important to the grilling process as is the preparation. The only fish I grill in fillet form is salmon. If you have your temp just right (I shoot for a hand thermometer reading of 'moderate'), the fish will cook thoroughly without needing to be turned at all. When it flakes easily with a fork, you're done. It also helps to keep the skin ON your fillets. This way, you don't lose any meat because it stuck to the grill, and it will peel off easily when the meat is done. With most other fish, I use the 'head and gut' method. Even though you have to deal with bones, there is so much less meat wasted using this method, and grilling is a snap, as the skin keeps the meat from searing to the grill, making for much easier turning.

Other seafood can be much less or ridiculously more demanding, depending on its type. Shellfish are simple to deal with, because the shell keeps you from having to scrape fishy bits off the grill. Squid, which has a texture unlike most other seafood, cooks almost instantaneously, and is very easy to turn to charred rubber. Needless to say, I do my best to avoid it at all costs. If you want tube and tentacle, go for deep-frying, and plan to make a little marinara sauce for dipping.

Cleaning and Scaling

Fish scales are no fun. You're going to be dealing with bones, anyway, so why worry about spitting scales all through dinner? Wipe the fish down from head to tail (to avoid getting stuck by any of the fins), wash it with a little water, and then pat it dry. Grip the fish tightly by the tail and, with the dull edge of a knife, scrape the scales from tail to head. It's best to warn bystanders, as the scales will tend to fly in unpredictable ballistic trajectories. When you've scraped the entire fish, wash it with a little water and wipe it from head to tail again. Now you're ready to get to the really gross part. . .

Refer to the picture below for reference. You should start with an exceptionally sharp knife. This being said, **great care should be taken to ensure the only thing that gets cut is the fish**! The first cut should be made on the underside of the fish, from about the gills to the vent (the exhaust port, if you will). Then, begin the second cut with the knife behind the pectoral fin, angling in toward the head. You are not cutting the head *off*, as much as severing the muscle and bone around it. This cut will meet the first cut on both sides and continue around the top of the fish, just severing the spine. Inspect the cut to be certain the head is free of the body and then, with a gentle twisting motion, remove the head (pulling it in the direction of the first cut). If this is done properly, the entrails should come out cleanly. Rinse out the cavity and start thinking about how you want to cook it!

Cut #2 should be behind the pectoral fin at an angle in toward the head. This cut will go from cut #1 around the top of the fish, just severing the backbone and continue on the other side, back down to cut #1 again.

Cut #1 should be from just behind the gills to the vent, right between the pelvic fins.

Crayfish Boil

While on a camping trip in Northern Michigan, we happened upon a stream with an abundant amount of crayfish. It turns out my son is pretty proficient at catching the little guys by hand. Before too long, we had a rather large bucketful and decided that it was a perfect day for a crayfish boil! Crayfish boils are usually huge (most recipes call for 30-60 lbs. of crayfish), but if you just want to cook up a mess to have with potatoes, that's fine too! Now, if you can believe it, not all of my family is hot on seafood, so I keep my recipes small. During this little camping excursion, we basically just boiled a mess of crayfish and baked some potatoes to go along. The recipe that follows is a bit more involved, but it will heartily feed a good-sized group.

Now, they don't call them 'mudbugs' for nothing, so care has to be taken in both their preparation and eating. For starters, you want to rinse them in salty water, usually about a couple of cups of salt to a cooler full of water. The salt will actually cause them to purge themselves of impurities, but you don't want to let them purge too long, as you do not want to boil dead crayfish.

Campfire Crayfish Boil

At least 5 lbs. of cleaned, live crayfish
4 Cloves garlic, sliced
4-5 oz. fresh mushrooms, sliced
6-8 Decent-sized red potatoes
1 Lb. smoked sausage, cut into coins
4 Celery ribs, sliced
2 Large onions cut into quarters
1 Lemon, halved
6 Ears of corn, shucked and halved
1¼ Cup Creole seasoning
2 Bay leaves

Creole Seasoning

2 Tbsp. Onion Powder
2 Tbsp. Garlic Powder
2 Tbsp. Oregano
2 Tbsp. Basil
1 Tbsp. Thyme
1 Tbsp. Black Pepper
1 Tbsp. White Pepper
1 Tbsp. Cayenne Pepper
5 Tbsp. Paprika
3 Tbsp. Salt

Using a large pot or turkey fryer, fill with water, mixing in creole seasoning, bay leaves, garlic, celery, onions, and lemon, and then bring it to a boil. Add potatoes and let cook for about 5 minutes. Add the mushrooms and sausage and cook for another 2 minutes. Add the corn and bring it back to a boil. Give the crayfish a final rinse, checking for and discarding any that are dead, then add the crayfish to the pot and bring it to a rolling boil. Turn off the heat and let them soak about 10 minutes before draining and serving.

Bob Wilkins

Winter Camping!

Yes, you *can* camp in the winter. No, I'm *not* making this up. Shortly before and for quite a while after we were married, Kim and I actually preferred camping in the 'off season'. Even if you are in a campground, the simple fact that fewer people are around gives you the feel of being alone in the wilderness, plus you have the added benefits of no bugs and fewer fuzzies. Now, fire does still work in winter, and keeping it burning is going to be more important to you when the temperature is 30° than it was when it was 80°. Warm water means cocoa and teas, and a crackling fire means you can warm yourself with a hot meal when the situation calls for it.

Fire-roasted potatoes and grilled salmon are a great combination when the temperature dips low. On this particular day, the fish started to freeze while I was preparing the fire!

Growing up, I had a fire pit in our back yard and, on occasion, I would make my own meals, regardless of the time of year. I started with things like burgers and smoked sausage, but as I grew old enough for my first part-time job, I began experimenting with things that were a bit more difficult, like Cornish game hens. Every now and again, my friend, Travis, would come by and we'd throw something together. Once, it was cold enough that we were warming ourselves on the steam rising from our baked potatoes!

Speaking of Which. . . Campfire Roasted Potatoes

One good-sized potato for each person to be fed
Butter
Salt & Pepper

Puncture the potato a few times with a fork and smear about 1 Tbsp. butter all over it, then wrap the potato tightly in aluminum foil. Place potatoes in hot coals for about 30-60 minutes (this is the tricky part, as a freakishly hot fire will char the potato's skin while leaving the center raw). Remove from the fire and carefully unwrap them, adding butter and seasoning to your taste.

Homesteader Potato

The homesteader is a little secret weapon of mine when I need something easy that makes people really feel they've been fed. Start out with:

- One good-sized potato for each person
- Small sizzler or chuck-eye steak per potato
- One medium onion, sliced into rings
- Butter
- Sour Cream
- Chives
- Shredded Cheese (sharp cheddar, Monterrey jack, or a combination of both)
- Salt
- Seasoned Pepper
- Cayenne Pepper

Puncture the potato a few times with a fork and smear about 1 Tbsp. butter all over it, then wrap it tightly in aluminum foil. Place the potatoes in hot coals for 30-60 minutes, dependent on fire temperature.

While the potatoes are cooking:

Sautee the onions in butter until they begin to get tender.

Grill your steaks to desired doneness, seasoning with salt and seasoned pepper, to taste.

Cut steak into cubes and keep warm in a small pan over the coolest side of your cook fire or grill.

Unwrap potato and mash open on a plate, adding butter, steak, sour cream, chives, and sprinkle (to taste) with cayenne pepper. Mix it all up and sprinkle generously with shredded cheese.

One should note that the homesteader is as open to experimentation as anything else in this book. In another variation, I sauté the onions with mushrooms in red wine, sprinkled with seasoned pepper. This may be a little complex for campfire cooking, but works well when at home, when you want an impressive, yet simply made meal for family and friends.

This little pile of potatoey goodness originally came to me on a biking/backpacking trip with a couple of friends through central Kentucky. We were all equipped with MREs (Meal Ready to Eat), but for the first night out, we actually each carried in a small steak and potato kit (soft-sided coolers are awesome, by the way). Once we got everything cooked, we realized that all we had to eat from were our mess kits, which afforded little room for knife work. The solution, of course, was to cut the steaks into little bits and mash it up together into our pans for shoveling. A day's worth of biking, followed by a hearty meal around the campfire and some horror stories (such as *The Backpacker and the Baby Food*) made for a fulfilling night.

Foiled Again!

As a rule, when you cook with foil, it should be three times the width of the food you're cooking. Fold the foil over and roll up the leading edges first, then the sides. This actually creates little steam pockets, which help cook the food more thoroughly. It should also be noted that, with the exception of baked potatoes, all foil cooking is done exclusively on a flameless fire—nothing but embers.

- Form a decent-sized hamburger patty and place it on a piece of foil with a potato cut into strips and an onion cut into rings. Season with salt and pepper and then fold the foil into a pocket. Cook on coals for 15 minutes.
- Smear an ear of corn with butter and wrap in a foil pocket. It will cook in about 10 minutes.
- Fruit can be baked easily in foil. Bananas usually take a little less than ten minutes. Apples will bake in 25-30. *Don't forget the cinnamon and nutmeg for this one!*

Moving On. . .

By now, you've probably noticed that I could go on and on about camp cooking. We could spend time talking about caveman roasts, and skewered birds, and all sorts of complicated things to do with fire and food, and even aluminum foil, but the fact of the matter is, *the simpler you keep it, the better off you will be.* Seriously, who wants to go camping and actually *worry* about things? Experiment! Try new things! It's fine if you fail (you *did* remember a backup plan, right?), because you still learned something.

The one, final thing I will leave you with for camping is dessert. Why would you go to all the trouble to cook in the wilderness and have nothing more for dessert than a marshmallow on a stick? A *burning* marshmallow, no less. I have no idea who came up with the idea of S'mores, but they were the perfect mixture of genius and sadist. Have you ever tried to *eat* one of those things? It's a great concept, since most everyone likes graham crackers, marshmallows, and chocolate, however, the marshmallow is usually the temperature and consistency of molten lava when you are trying to sandwich it all together.

Pack a waffle-style ice cream cone with mini marshmallows, banana slices, and chocolate bits (chocolate chips or a cut-up candy bar will do), and wrap it tightly with aluminum foil. Stick the whole thing over hot coals for about 5 minutes, turning occasionally. Let it cool a bit after you unwrap it, and enjoy your s'more cone with relatively clean hands!

Chapter VIII

Survival!

The crisp, autumn day starts out with abundant sunshine and a hearty breakfast. You break camp and head off to find adventure on what you expected to be a long, but easy to navigate trail. A few hours in, you realize that, somewhere along the way, you got onto an animal trail; probably back in that maple grove covered in newly-fallen leaves. Your mind starts to race a little. *How long have I been off the trail? Landmarks! Did I pass anything memorable on the way here*? Looking back, the path you followed is harder to see than it was coming here; a trick of light and shadow, now that the sun has moved significantly lower in the sky. Still, you try to retrace your steps, consulting your compass every so often, but now you're following a gulley and have no idea even where the animal trail has gotten to. The sun will be setting soon, and your mind turns to one thought; *autumn in bear country.*

To be thrust into a life-or-death situation can be a scary prospect. Just hearing the word 'survival' conjures many images; from being a hiker, lost and separated from your group, to being stuck at home with no water or power because of some natural disaster. Obviously, the latter would be the best position to be in, as there would most likely be neighbors in the same situation to come together as a group for support. One of the worst scenarios would be someone on their own in the middle of nowhere with nothing but the contents of their pockets for resources. Let's face it, not many people carry MREs and water filtration straws around with them. If you were in a bad situation, either alone or with a group, would you know how to find water? How would you make a shelter? How would you find food?

The answer to all of these depends solely upon location. Knowing something about the area you will be going to will give you an edge when it comes to locating resources. Finding water in a boreal forest is much easier than, say, the desert. Shelter too, as a matter of fact. Food is another matter entirely. For the most part, animals are edible, though the problem with hunting is that you have to actually *find and catch them*. That involves a time-consuming process that burns precious calories that you need to conserve. Insects and arachnids are possibilities as well, but you need to know which ones are poisonous. Plants will put a world of hurt on you if you do not know which ones are edible, and by all that is holy, you should *avoid mushrooms*!

There are a few things you should keep in mind as you read this chapter:

- **This is NOT a definitive guide to survival**. Yes, I have had survival training and what follows is good stuff, however, survivalists more knowledgeable than I have written books in excess of 300-500 pages long and that **still may not help your particular situation**! The fact of the matter is, you never know what might happen to you, and the book that would be so helpful in any other part of the world may be nothing but fire starting material in your particular location.
- **Know your limitations**. Let's face it, some people could read all the books and take all the classes in the world on survival, hunting, building shelters, etc., and still not survive a night in the woods if they had the Army National Guard in their hip pocket. The first rule of survival is to do your best *not* to get into a survival situation, especially if you couldn't start a fire with five gallons of gasoline and a flame thrower.
- **Seeking out knowledge is important**. Read about and talk to people who are experienced in the area to which you are traveling. You wouldn't think of driving three states over for a hunting trip and just wandering into an unknown section of woods, would you?
- **Know about the area in which you live**. I've known people who have lived in an area all their lives and never explored more than a few miles

from their home. Knowing the resources available where you live will increase your chances of surviving the aftermath of a natural disaster or service breakdown.

- **Be prepared**. The old Boy Scout Motto comes in handy in all facets of life. It's amazing how many people will go on a wilderness hike without even giving the slightest thought to potential disaster. *Did you remember a compass*? I always carry a small survival tin, even when I'm hunting in a very familiar area. Gadgetry and supplies aside, you have to remember that the one thing you always have to depend on in a survival situation is *yourself*.

Water!

In the camping chapter, we discussed the most basic things you need to provide: Fire, shelter, water, and food. Well, the idea behind camping is that you are *prepared* to spend time in the wilderness. You either are carrying in the supplies you need, or you know where to get them at your destination. When disaster strikes, you don't always have the luxury of a full water bottle or canteen at the ready. In a *survival* situation, things are a bit different on the priorities list. Now, the big three are:

- Water
- Fire
- Shelter

"Wait," you may say, "why isn't food on the list?" The thing is, despite what we all might think, humans are capable of surviving for better than three weeks without food, but three days without water can be a deadly situation. Depending on the environment, you would start feeling the effects of dehydration after 24 hours, with loss of coordination and severe headaches hampering any of your efforts to stay alive.

There are myriad ways to collect water, but how many will work for you is completely dependent on the environment in which you find yourself and how well you are equipped. If you are out in the wilderness in the winter, it could be as easy as melting snow, or you could be in the desert, trying to dodge scorpions as you dig a hole for a solar still. A simple solution for most hikers and backpackers would be a filter straw, which can be purchased for around $20. They are small, lightweight, easily packed, and allow the user to drink from most water sources without trepidation. Other options are water purification tablets and rudimentary water filters, which are fashioned from fabric and the materials at hand in the wild. Purification tablets will kill most waterborne pathogens, but take some time to work. Any water filter you may be able to construct in the wild (and there is a litany of instructions to be found online for them) will only filter out turbidity. Anything like giardia or cryptosporidium will still be swimming around in there, eager to make the rest of your adventure that much more horrible. **It should be noted that water purification devices, chemical treatments, and boiling may remove *biological* contaminants, but will do little to remove *chemical* contaminants!** This is where knowing something about your area comes into play. If you are lost in an area that was the site of extensive mining, some form of industry, is prone to naturally occurring contamination, or downstream from anything of a toxic nature, distilling your drinking water may be a very good idea.

Though we travel quite a bit, the areas we frequent are most often forested regions. I've used a couple of different versions of solar stills that work very well (provided you have the foresight to carry a clear, plastic bag in your kit).

The vegetation still, pictured on the following page, is an excellent way to gather some extra water if you are in an area lush with greenery. Of course, the stranded adventurer needs to be certain not to use poisonous plants in its construction. Solar stills have the advantage of generating water that is free of contaminants, regardless of the quality of water you have to start with. Urine can be adequately recycled using a still. The problem with solar stills, though, is time. In ideal conditions, a still will generate about a quart of water every 24 hours. The human body (again, depending upon the environment) needs about *two* quarts of water per day, on average, to remain healthy. This means that, among all of the other factors you have to pay attention to while surviving, you have to be conscious of your hydration level and limit your activity as best you can to keep from using too much water.

Typical vegetation still—A clear, plastic bag is used to contain as many branches of a handy tree as possible (left); After tying the bag tightly, it will condense water from the vegetation, esp. in direct sunlight (center); Note a rock has been used to create a low spot in which water may gather (right)

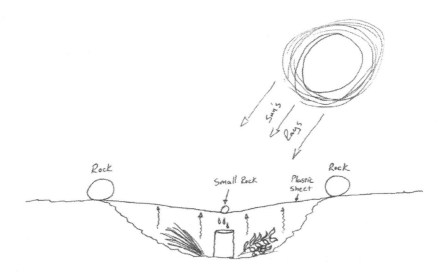

Another type of still is made from a hole dug in the ground. Plastic sheeting is anchored around the hole and a rock is used to create a drip point in the center, over a cup or other container. Vegetation is then added to help the process along. Urine or other contaminated water may also be used to moisten the ground, speeding condensation.

The best possible way to monitor your fluid loss is, of course, by paying attention to your urination. If your urine is clear, or looks like pale lemonade, you are still hydrated. The darker the liquid gets, the worse off you are, plus, you will be going less frequently. The early symptoms of dehydration are thirst and decreased urine output. As the condition progresses, the mouth becomes dry and the eyes stop making tears. If you stop sweating, even in extreme heat, this is a sign that you need water *immediately*! Further symptoms include muscle cramps, nausea, dizziness, heart palpitations, severe weakness, and the end-all, be-all symptom: death.

Fire!

Fire is, without a doubt, the most useful thing to have when stuck in the wilderness. It will give you light, heat, a means to cook, the ability to dry out when you get wet, and will go a fair way towards keeping animals out of your camp. Fire can also put a world of hurt upon you if you do not respect it or know what you are doing, and it is also extremely difficult to make. Learning to make fire by several methods ensures that you will be at least partially prepared for any situation you encounter. How do you make fire in the rain, or a rain-soaked forest? For that matter, how do you build a fire when there are two or more feet of snow all around you? Those are difficult enough to answer now; how about when your life depends on it?

Fire-starting tools →

- Butane Lighter
- Matches (of any variety)
- Ferro Rod
- Magnesium Fire Starter

Handy Bits to Have Around →

- Petroleum Jelly-Soaked Cotton Balls
- Dryer Fluff
- Pencil Sharpener (no, really!)
- Sharp Knife

The seasoned adventurer and novice, alike, should always prepare for the worst. Cotton balls soaked with petroleum jelly are easy to pack, and will generally burn between 5-10 minutes, when lit. Keeping a butane lighter on hand is a great idea, but what if it runs out of fuel or gets lost? My favorite go-to is the magnesium fire starter. It is, basically, a block of magnesium with a ferro stick attached to the back side. When ignited, magnesium burns at 5610°F! At that temperature, even wet tinder doesn't stand much of a chance. We'll go through some fire starting methods in a bit. First, we should look at fire *safety*.

How NOT to get burned →

As we mentioned in the Camping section (Chapter 7, for those not paying attention), care must be taken when you embark upon the task of lighting a fire. All of the methods and tools mentioned here are tried and true, but if you are careless or just don't know what you are doing, you can injure yourself, touch off a wildfire, die, or at least burn off your eyebrows. Just because you are lost in the wilderness and need to make a fire to live doesn't mean you can ignore these possibilities. I've known seasoned outdoor enthusiasts and survival experts that have nearly *burned down their own shelter* because they became complacent with their fires. That being said, we will spend a second or two going over a few things we talked about before, just in case you may have skimmed over it.

Firstly, you should always check for:

- Dry leaves or needles
- Dry grasses
- Low-hanging trees, especially evergreens
- Steady or gusting winds
- Garbage or other human detritus

Always remember to clear any burnable material out to a radius of several feet from your fire, to avoid the possibility of touching off another blaze. I've been in forests where the ground is thick with pine needles to the point of feeling like a mattress. If a random spark touches off something like that, you are going to find yourself in a much more dangerous situation than you started with.

Starting fires in wet or snowy areas →

Neither of these is a fun situation to be in. You are wet, cold, most likely shivering, and you need to build a fire. This is where some advance planning comes in. I mentioned dryer fluff and petroleum jelly cotton balls a little ways back. Both of these items will help you in damp situations, but not before you've prepared your fire lay. In snowy areas, your only chance is to dig down to ground level, as close as you can manage, and build a foundation out of rocks or wood to keep your fire off of the wet earth.

In wet conditions, your best hope lies in your tinder and kindling. If you are in a downpour, you may have to accept the fact that fire isn't going to happen; at least, not right away. Spend time collecting *quality* tinder. This is the time when you shouldn't rush things, as it's your tinder and small, pencil-thin fuel that is going to warm up and, hopefully, dry out your larger fuel which will sustain the fire. Dry plants, shaved tree bark, and old man's beard all make excellent tinder, assuming you find some dry enough to light. If your tinder is a little damp, shoving it in your pocket to allow your body heat to dry it while you gather larger wood is an option. For larger fuel, you may have to get creative, especially if the area you're in is sodden from hours' or days' worth of rain. Remember, too, that wet wood may not be wet all the way through! You may find dry wood by splitting larger pieces to get to their cores (you *did* bring a good knife, right?).

Determining the best fire lay to use is no different than if you are in a camping situation. If you need to shelter your fire from wind or rain, the Hunter's fire lay is the best, especially if it starts raining heavily and you need to cover your coals to keep the fire bed hot and dry. If you need to dry out quickly, a larger, tipi-style fire lay or reflector lay are your best bets.

Once your fire lay is established, you can make use of some of the handy items in your kit. Dryer fluff (cleaned out of your dryer's lint trap) is an excellent fire starter, as it is made up of small, very flammable cotton or polyester fibers. Pull it apart a little, set a flame to it, and it will burn in a steady manner. Remembering to bring some in a little zipper bag is much easier than trying to mine your navel for fuzz nuggets. As far as the pencil sharpener goes, it is a simple item that can be had for less than a buck from most department stores (make sure you get one that will sharpen the big elementary school pencils). It will shave a nice, thin ribbon of tinder from the ends of your sticks that can easily cut your foraging time significantly. Of note: it will also leave you with a sharpened stick that can be used for a small animal trap, arrow, or spear!

Reflector Fire Lay with Shelter

A reflector fire lay makes use of either a natural or constructed backstop to redirect the heat that would normally escape away from your shelter. Suitable backstops would be large rocks, a wall of stones, stacked logs, an emergency blanket, or a wall of logs braced on branches driven in the ground (as shown in the sketch on page 75). If you choose to make a reflector out of material that could burn or melt, care should be taken to both keep the fire away from it and to not let it get too large. You should also keep in mind the fact that any shelter you build will be prone to burning, as well. I've known a few outdoor enthusiasts who have tried to build their fire either too close to the entrance, or *inside* the shelter. They went to great lengths to create a vent and chimney to allow the smoke to be drawn out, and also kept the fire very tiny. The problem with this method is, the chimney causes a draft through the shelter which robs you of needed warmth, and keeping a fire small enough to not be a danger to your shelter requires a lot of tending, robbing you of needed rest. Add to that the fact that, in two such instances, these guys *set fire to their shelters*! Needless to say, I do <u>NOT</u> recommend building your fire very close, much less inside with you. When properly positioned, a reflector fire will make for a very warm shelter. When adequate bedding is established to insulate yourself from the ground, even an extremely cold night can be rendered tolerable.

A few, quick notes about sleeping warm—there are a few things you need to remember, should you not be able to build a fire or environmental conditions render your fire ineffective:

1. **Keep your feet warm by wearing a hat**—We all have that mother or grandmother that chased us down if we left the house without a hat. Turns out that she was right; we lose a large amount of heat from our heads.
2. **Go to bed with a snack**—If you have carb-heavy food available, such as energy bars or fatty snacks (remember the pemmican recipe?), have a little before you bed down, to keep your internal temperature up.
3. **Warm up before lying down**—Light exercise, like pushups or jumping jacks will raise your internal temperature before hunkering down for the night, but *don't overdo it*! You need to stop short of causing yourself to sweat, or you will make your situation worse.
4. **Keep hydrated**—Your body works best when hydrated. That includes the internal furnace.
5. **Change clothes**—If you are fortunate enough to have extra clothing, change into something dry before bedding down. What you've been

wearing during the day is likely to be damp, which will rob you of heat as you sleep.

6. **Don't be shy about that water bottle**—Backpackers know the value of placing a hot water bottle in their sleeping bag for extra warmth. The water warms the inside of the bag and acts as a thermal mass. In a survival situation you may be limited on ways to heat water, but there are alternatives. Though it may seem somewhat revolting, if you are in a desperate enough situation and need help keeping your temperature up, urinating into your water bottle or another handy watertight container will help warm things up (the human body runs around 98°, internally). The main thing here is **do NOT forget to rinse it out before using it for drinking water again! URINE IS *NOT* FOR DRINKING!**

Shelter!

I could easily write an entire book on the subject of building a shelter in the wilderness. For brevity's sake, I am not going to do that. Here, we will just look at some of the basic points for shelter *selection*. Learning how to build a shelter, like anything else, is a matter of taking the time to learn and practice the skill. The issue of shelter can be the simplest, yet most overthought obstacle to overcome in a survival situation. The first thing most people forget, whether through panic or just lack of experience, is to **build from the ground up**. *Many a person has worked for hours trying to get a roof over their head, then spent the night freezing on the cold ground because they neglected to think about their bedding.* When you find it necessary to hunker down and begin construction, how do you decide from the litany of methods which is best? Before you settle on any of them, there are a few things you must consider:

- **Availability of materials**. Obviously, you will have more options in a forest than you would in a desert, but you also have to remember to think *simply*. Shelter is a game of opportunity, just as much as is foraging for food. Digging a shelter out of deep snow makes for a cozy spot, if you do it the proper way. Caves, overhangs, and fallen or uprooted trees can provide shelter in a pinch, saving you from expending unnecessary calories in a search to obtain building materials. If night is closing in fast, scuffling into a pile of leaves and forest loam/humus could provide the insulation you need to survive the night.
- **What are you protecting yourself from**? Is it cold where you are stranded? Is it raining endlessly? Are wild animals a potential threat?

All of these must be considered when thinking about shelter. In the desert, shelter means shade during the day and insulation against the cold nights. A cave or rock overhang will do against rain in a pinch, or a densely layered roof of evergreen boughs covering a stick frame. Smallish wild animals may be kept at bay by a fire, but you might need to build a barricade to keep larger predators from getting too close. Bugs? Forget it. Bugs are going to get in, no matter what you do, but elevated bedding will keep the ground-based crawlies to a minimum.

- **Safety**! Having to survive in the wilderness is bad enough without unwittingly putting yourself in a worse situation. Older forests are full of trees that could break in a high wind. While rock overhangs may act as heat sinks, collecting the heat of the sun or your fire and re-radiating it, quickly heating a cold rock could cause it to crack, leaving you with a minivan-sized stone inconveniently tumbling down upon your head. Do you remember that cave we talked about before? Did you think to check it for bears or other unsavory critters before you walked/crawled in?

- **Duration**. How long will you need your shelter? If the odds are high that you will be rescued tomorrow, or you are simply waiting out the night, would you spend three hours building a shelter, or just crawl up into a pile of leaves for warmth? Are you in an area with abundant water and food sources and plenty of open visibility for rescue, or are you in a deep gulch with little vegetation, too many bugs, and nothing but soggy mud?

One of the hardest decisions you could ever have to make in any survival situation is to keep moving or to hunker down. If you hunker down, you are, basically, deciding that your best chance of being found is to wait for help to come to you. Rescue is your ultimate goal, so you must put yourself in a position to best achieve it. The main thing to keep in mind is to *make yourself as visible as possible*! When you build a shelter out of indigenous materials, you are camouflaging yourself from possible rescuers, so steps must be taken to make your base camp stand out to passers-by or search aircraft. The decision to move on cannot be taken lightly, either. Getting to higher ground will limit your ability to find water and food, possibly put you in a much colder and less sheltered environment, and could cause you to leave behind some of your gear, whether through necessity or accidental loss. We could go on and on here, so for the sake of brevity, we'll assume you've decided to stay put. . .

Finding Your Next Meal

Your shelter is built, you found a mountain stream nearby, and you have a fire that will boil your water and keep you warm through the night; now it's time to think about possibly eating something. Depending on what the environment presents to you and the equipment you have at hand, you have three main choices:

- **Fishing**—Easy, if you have the right tools with which to work, fishing will provide protein with possibly the least amount of spent calories, as you do not have to stalk your prey or walk around setting a ridiculous amount of snares and traps (though fish traps *are* something you might think about). Fish are easy to clean with a good knife, and may be smoked over the fire to preserve the meat for several days.
- **Hunting/Trapping**—Hunting and trapping requires a bit of thought and some measure of experience. Between the two, trapping is the best way to catch your quarry, as you only need to sniff out the animals' trails and dens. Ideally, you would lay out as many snares as possible and then return later to (hopefully) harvest your game. Small game can be easily cooked over the fire, but care should be taken to *make certain it is cooked completely*, since your already bad situation would be made that much worse by food poisoning or parasites.
- **Foraging**—Once again, I cannot stress enough how easily you can get into trouble eating plants, if you do not know how to identify them. This is one of those times when knowing your area can pay off. Wild edibles may be light on calories, but learning how to properly graze will keep you going, despite lack of animals to cook. Foraging doesn't just mean looking for edible plants—insects and arachnids are fair game, too, provided you know which ones are safe.

Through it all, you should also keep in mind this one, main rule of thumb: ***Do not attempt to eat something that can eat you back***! Larger animals, swarming insects, and venomous snakes are but a few of the menu selections you should probably avoid. This sounds like a no-brainer, I know, but desperation has pushed many a rational person to thinking that the most ridiculous notion is a pretty good idea. Basically, if it sounds like it would make a good scene in an action movie, you probably shouldn't attempt it. With all of that in mind, let's go find something for dinner. . .

Bringing the Food to You. . .

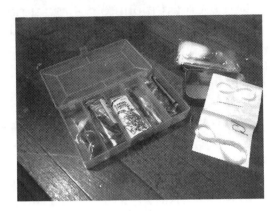

When out in the wilderness, whether by design or by chance, you have limited supplies, if any at all. Caloric energy is at a premium, so you want to minimize the amount of effort it takes to do *anything*, even when gathering food. Active hunting expends the most energy, as it usually involves stalking and sometimes running after game. Fishing is easy enough, if you have a good spot available and the proper equipment. Any adventurer worthy of the name carries a small kit in his or her bag. Pictured above is the kit I keep in my backpack, with a small supply of line, hooks, sinkers, floats, and even some artificial bait. The smaller box next to it is a pocket survival kit, fashioned from a candy tin, which has a small fishing kit and a few other survival necessities (you *are* getting the hang of this whole "be prepared for the worst" theme, right?). With a kit like this, fishing is made quite a bit easier, though it is a bit tricky to catch fish without a pole, as so many of us are used to using. Another method would be to set a "Fish Trap", and let the little guys come to you.

A simple Fish Trap

A fish trap is, basically, a barricade that is made from sticks, logs, or rocks that will snare fish in tight quarters, making them easier to catch. The diagram here shows what I like to call a "mushroom trap", which has worked well for me in trout streams. The idea is that fish will swim into the trap and have a difficult time finding the exit. With the fish gathered in such a tight area, a makeshift net or spear will make short work of them. A net can be fashioned from the shirt off your back, and you should already have a spear (since you remembered to bring your pencil sharpener to help make fire starting tinder). One should remember that water *refracts* light, much like a lens. Attempting to spear a fish may result in a miss, until you learn to compensate.

Another type of fish trap involves creating a barrier the width of the stream with a gathering area in the center, into which you can "drive" the fish. This type of trap is time consuming to build and works much better if you have someone to assist.

Utilizing the same philosophy on land, a sharp-eyed adventurer should be able to spot trails frequented by animals and set snares that will do the hunting for them. Pictured below are some snare uses that I have found effective in a number of situations. The snares can be made with paracord, monofilament, rope, or wire, though the latter is the most workable of all of these.

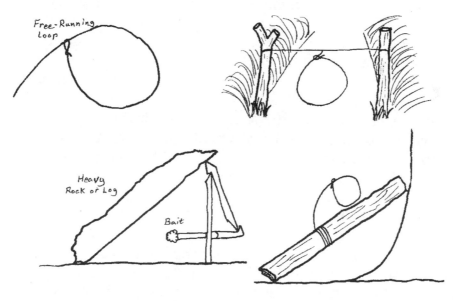

Common Snares and Traps

Okay, you've caught something—now what? Fish are simple to clean with a little practice, using the method we discussed in the camping chapter. In a survival situation, picking around a few bones is nothing compared to the sorrow of wasted meat if you were to attempt to fillet your catch. You have no idea when you might get to eat next, so it is imperative that you utilize every morsel. Once you've gutted the fish, cooking is a simple matter, as you can "fry" it on a flat rock by the fire, or just jam a stick in its mouth and suspend it over the flames. With a little preparation, you can smoke fish to make it last longer. This is time consuming, requiring that you construct a "smoke box" out of indigenous materials or something from your kit (rain poncho, tarp, emergency blanket, etc.). The idea is to keep the smoke in on the meat, so your box will need to be draft-proof. Occasionally adding some green wood to the fire or small pieces of cedar boughs will keep the smoke going. Suspend the fish at least 12 inches above the flames and hunker down, because the process takes all day. The fish is done when the skin peels off easily and the meat flakes.

Small game is a bit more complicated and messy to prepare, but as with anything else, practice shortens the effort. Assuming you don't catch anything like porcupine or armadillo, cleaning small game uses generally the same method, regardless of the animal. In a nutshell:

1. Kill the animal in the most humane way possible. If you've caught something in a snare and it's still alive, a sharp blow to the base of the skull will sever the spine and end things quickly.
2. Remove the paws and the head. There isn't any meat on either, and it will make removing the pelt that much easier.
3. Pinch up some of the skin on the back and make a cut along the spine, cutting through the skin, only.
4. In most small animals, the skin will peel off like a coat. Keep your knife handy to cut any membranes that may hamper its removal. If you removed the paws, it will pull right off both hind and forelegs.
5. Feel for the bottom of the ribcage and carefully make a shallow cut downward to expose the internal organs. If you cut too deeply, you may slice into the digestive organs or the urine sack, ruining the meat. The organ cavity of most wild animals does not have the most pleasing smell—this is not an indication that the meat is bad; it's just wild game. Insert two fingers into the ribcage and scoop out the organs. The heart, liver, and kidneys are all edible; the rest should be thrown away (or used as bait for your next meal).

6. Rinse the carcass thoroughly and put it to the fire. Remember, you should always thoroughly cook any wild meat to ensure your ordeal isn't further complicated by parasites or other foodborne pathogens.

Cleaning game can sound and look very easy when someone else is doing it. Do not be discouraged if your first time ends up looking like more of a bloodbath than the average 80's action film. I was lucky enough to see several squirrels and rabbits cleaned before I tried my hand at it. By the time I held the knife, I had already developed an opinion of a couple of tried and true methods and did very well for myself. In a survival skills course, I actually ate very well because of a rabbit warren that was not too far from what our instructor called the "marooning point" of the expedition.

As with anything else in life, you can get too much of a good thing. Rabbit meat (and squirrel, to a lesser degree) is exceptionally lean—ridiculously so. Can you ever think of a time you saw a fat rabbit? *Rabbit Starvation* is a term for a type of malnutrition the body experiences when all you ingest are proteins. Symptoms of this condition include headaches, fatigue, diarrhea, slow heart rate, and a hunger that can only be sated by consuming fats or carbohydrates. Rabbit meat generally has about 7-8% fat against a roughly 20% protein content. Compare that to beef, which is usually in the 30% fat content and 15-16% protein area and you can see where the balanced fat/protein issue becomes sketchy. Remember pemmican, our "survival superfood"? That is about 50% fat. The lesson to be learned here is that nothing is ever easy. Just because you can eat it, doesn't mean it will keep you healthy.

Other Issues—

We've spoken a little about *eating* wild animals, but we should also take some time to discuss *protecting yourself from some of them*. Just as much as you are looking for a good meal, nature will, to varying degrees which depend on your location, attempt to eat you, too. Bears are inherently curious and usually always hungry. Whether or not they think you would make a tasty snack, they will cause all manner of grief to the hapless traveler. A while back, someone once told me of a game camera he lost because he forgot to wash his hands after eating a fast food burger and then setting it up at his deer blind.

If you are lost in an area populated by large predators (bear, wolves, coyotes, cougars, etc.), you should always be careful with how you handle your foodstuffs.

We've all heard the "hang your foods from a tree" method to keep bears out of the camp grub, but it's also a very good idea to prepare and cook your food *away from your campsite*. The smell from cooking game and fish linger long after the meal has been eaten. The absolute last thing you want to wake up to in the dark of the night is a large predator sniffing around because you cooked those lucky trout in the fire three feet from your shelter entrance!

Small nuisances can become large problems, as well. If you are out in the wild, the only thing that will keep you totally bug-free is cold weather. Ergo, if you are out in the warmer, non-wintery months, improperly discarded or stored foodstuffs will attract insects. Black flies are bad enough in the northern tier of the United States without an added excuse for them to be around. Ants can also become a large issue. All it takes is one scout to find something you've stashed away that it thinks is beneficial for the entire colony to beat a path to your door.

All this being said, here is some general, common sense to keep in mind:

- When you set up camp, check the area for animal trails, tracks, insect nests/hills.
- Clean and cook any fish or game away from your camp (at least 100 yards, if possible) if the area you're in is prone to predatory animals.
- The smell of cooking lingers on skin and clothing, as well. Wash your hands after eating, if possible, and do your best to not sleep in the clothing you wore while cooking. *Do not bring the smell of cooking back to your shelter*!
- **NEVER** bring food back to your shelter. If you are lucky enough to catch and smoke fish, do your best to find a place that predators cannot reach. Suspending it from a branch overhead (at least 10-15 feet high and 4-5 feet from the tree trunk) will usually suffice.

Survival is an iffy business. Nothing you can do will make it completely pleasurable to be lost in the wilderness, since most of your waking thoughts are going to be centered on the subject of not dying (it *is* the general definition of the word, after all). The best thing you can do is *arm yourself with as much knowledge and practical experience as you can* before going out hiking, hunting, camping, etc. **Don't just read about it. Practice it.** Find someone who is knowledgeable in the skills you want to develop and learn from them. Learning from someone with experience is the best way to keep from injuring yourself or someone else in the process. In the end, when you find yourself turned around in a snow-covered forest, you'll welcome the feeling of reason pushing away the panic as you begin to remember what you need to do.

CHAPTER IX

Some Closing Thoughts
and Adventures...

Show me a camper who hasn't first pitched his or her tent in the backyard, and I'll show you the person who will be the next dinner theatre attraction in the campground. Reading about how to make and use a fire bow will not properly prepare you for the ordeal (and blisters) of actually using one. Likewise, running a deep-fryer on your kitchen countertop can be a volatile affair, if you've never done it before. The best way to not have pictures of you in a flaming apron spread around the internet by your friends is to practice before your performance. Come to think of it, it might also be a good idea to have friends who will care enough to grab water, rather than their cameras (or baking soda, depending what you used to set yourself ablaze).

One of the things I first mentioned in this book was *creativity*. Every recipe in here was either inspired by something or someone, or was born from a stock of odd ingredients that I thought might actually collide well. Cooking for adults is bad enough; when you're cooking for multiple kids, you are entering a Def-Con One situation: Some like hot and spicy, some like a little heat, one likes totally mild seasoning, while yet another will eat beef liver, if it is prepared properly. The key to successful experimentation is to work with flavors you enjoy, but remember that not everyone might think your "Vindaloobecue" is a good idea without being served with a tall, frosty fire extinguisher. I came up with *Firecracker Chicken* after working a double shift and getting home well after dark. I had frozen chicken breasts and pasta, but didn't quite want a marinara. With just at 45 minutes before one of my favorite sci fi shows began, I decided to throw some new ingredients into the mix. The result was pleasantly warm and only required a sauté pan and a pot in which to boil the pasta.

Firecracker Chicken

2 Boneless, skinless chicken breasts
1 Sixteen ounce can of tomato sauce
1 Ten ounce can of diced tomatoes & chilies, drained*
4 Ounces chopped mushrooms
1 Medium onion, chopped
1 Cup small shells
1/3 Cup White wine
2 Tbsp. Olive Oil

To taste:

- Salt
- Seasoned pepper
- Rosemary
- Oregano
- Cilantro

In a 5 quart sauté pan, heat 1 tablespoon of olive oil and cook onions for one minute, stirring constantly. Add mushrooms, 1/3 cup white wine, and tomatoes & chilies. Reduce heat and simmer until wine has all but evaporated. Remove from heat and set aside.

Start pasta boiling.

In the sauté pan, heat 1 tablespoon of olive oil over medium heat and sauté chicken breasts, seasoning with seasoned pepper and rosemary. When chicken is cooked through, add tomato sauce, salt, oregano, cilantro, and reserved mushroom/onion/tomato mix. Stir thoroughly and simmer, covered, over low heat for about six to seven minutes.

* It should be noted that canned, diced tomatoes and chilies are also available in *mild*, should members of your audience like things a bit more on the tamer side.

On one particular dreary night, I ended up in another "whatchagot" situation with random ingredients and a bunch of "I don't know, what do you want" responses. This was a family movie night, so I, naturally, didn't want to be in the kitchen forever. Armed with a pork roast and various other little niceties, *Worcesteriqued Pork* came about.

Worcesteriqued Pork

1.5 lbs. pork (I used a pork roast, sliced into cutlets)
Teriyaki sauce
Worcestershire sauce
White wine vinegar
Any good barbeque sauce
Garlic and Herb seasoning (available just about anywhere)

Sautee the cutlets in a shallow pan, with enough teriyaki sauce to cover the bottom. Sprinkle liberally with garlic and herb seasoning. The intent here is to whiten the meat, not cook it thoroughly. That comes later. Set aside when done.

In a mixing bowl, combine three tbsp. teriyaki sauce, one tbsp. Worcestershire sauce, one tbsp. white wine vinegar, and two tbsp. of any good barbeque sauce. Pour over meat and marinate for 15 minutes.

Place meat and marinade in a shallow baking pan, arranging so the cutlets are not touching one another, then cook for 25-30 minutes (or until done) at 350 degrees. *Note that your cooking time will increase if you use bone-in chops.*

I served these up with oven-roasted potatoes and garlic, but they will go with just about anything. They are even tender enough to serve as sandwiches.

Remember the Campfire Soup recipe back on page 56? Purely by accident, we discovered that it also made a nice stew. We were planning on having the soup after I got home from work, but during the cooking, my wife let it boil down, thickening it via reduction. She ended up having to add two cups of water twice during the cooking, as she reduced it nearly by ¾ both times. The total cooking time, once everything was in the pot, was approximately 3 hours. This extra time gave the potatoes (yes, we added those, too) plenty of time to soften, and the reduction process helped tenderize the beef in much the same way as Swiss steak.

Campfire *Stew*

3 Tbsp. butter
2 Large onions, chopped
1 Lb. bag of baby carrots, chopped
2 Celery ribs, sliced

2 13½ oz. cans of tomatoes OR 2 14 ½ oz. cans of diced tomatoes
1 10 oz. can diced tomatoes and chilies
2 Cups chicken stock
2 Tbsp. chopped basil
¼ Cup white wine (optional, though recommended)
1 Tsp. sugar
7 or 8 good sized red potatoes, roughly cubed
1.5 Lbs. stew meat or diced chuck steak

Melt 2 Tbsp. butter in a large pot over moderate heat. Brown the meat, seasoning with salt and pepper to taste. Remove from pot and set aside.

Melt remaining butter in pot, and then add onions, carrots, and celery, stirring constantly for 2 minutes.

Add wine and cook for another minute. Stir in the tomatoes (if you used whole canned tomatoes, mash them with the end of a wooden spoon).

Add stew meat, sugar, and stock, plus enough water to cover everything. Add potatoes and basil, then give it a good stir.

Bring to an *energetic* simmer at medium heat, reducing the broth by nearly ¾. Add 2 cups water and continue simmering until the broth reduces *again* by nearly ¾. Add 2 cups water and continue simmering, albeit a bit more slowly, for one hour, or until you've achieved your desired thickness.

Curry in a Hurry

My brief summer with Madhi, coupled with exposure to a British sci-fi comedy show, is what drove me into experimentation with Indian cuisine. Despite her tutelage, my first attempt at a basic curry was a disaster (though some of it had to do with the amount of seniority the curry powder in mom's spice rack had, I'm sure). Through and since my college years, I have developed a knack for fine-tuning those pungent and flavorful spices, from Tikka Masala to fiery Vindaloo. Sometimes, unfortunately, we don't always have the time to go all-out, so this simple "cheater" curry recipe was born out of necessity. As shown, this recipe will serve two, but upping the ante on the chicken and rice will feed however many you need. The broth to milk ratio is 1:1, so it is very easy to increase.

1 Tbsp. Olive Oil
½ Cup chicken broth
½ Cup milk
3-5 Tsp. red curry powder (to taste)
2 Tbsp. mango chutney (hot or mild)
Chili powder (to taste)
2 Boneless chicken breasts, cubed
1 Medium onion (yellow or white), chopped
1 Cup instant rice

Prepare rice per the package instructions.

Heat the oil in a sauté pan until it starts to shimmer, then cook the onion, stirring constantly, until it just becomes tender. Set the onion aside in a bowl and cook the chicken in the remaining olive oil, sprinkling with chili powder early on. Note that I said, "To taste". I turn the chicken *red* with chili powder, but that's me. Once the chicken is thoroughly cooked, remove it to the same bowl as the reserved onion.

If you haven't already, mix together the broth, milk, curry, and chutney, then add it to the pan, bringing it up to simmer over medium heat. You will want to be stirring occasionally, during the process. Once the sauce starts to simmer, add the chicken and onion, cooking for one minute more (back the heat down if it becomes too energetic).

Serve the curry over a bed of rice.

Even side items can be accentuated with the addition of simple spice cabinet contents. I come from a predominantly Southern background, so meat also becomes a seasoning, to some degree. There is nothing quite like a pot of garden-grown green beans that have been simmering on the stovetop for hours with a large ham hock in the pot. Cayenne pepper and seasoned salt blends are excellent as well, but don't forget the onions. Macaroni and cheese can be stepped up a bit, also, without the need for boxed mixes. This recipe has proven to be quite addictive to guests at our house.

Macaroni and Cheese

12 Oz. Pasta
1 Tbsp. Butter
1 Tsp. All-purpose flour
2 Cups Milk
2 Tsp. Worcestershire sauce
½ Tsp. Garlic powder
½ Tsp. Mustard powder
¼ Tsp. Salt
¼ Tsp. Pepper
2 Cups Shredded Cheddar

Boil and drain the pasta.

Melt the butter over low heat, then stir in the flour, cooking about 30 seconds. Stir in the remaining ingredients, except for the cheese, at medium heat. Simmer for one minute, then add 1 ½ cups of cheese. Stir in the pasta, then place in a baking dish. Spread remaining cheese on top and bake until the cheese starts to melt. If you want to brown the cheese a bit, one minute in the broiler will do.

> → To speed things up a bit when you are gathering your ingredients, everything in the list, from the milk to the pepper, can be mixed together in one 2 cup measure.

Before we go, I suppose dessert should get a mention (outside of the s'mores cones back when we were talking about camp cooking). I have never been great with desserts. I can make a cake or a pie, here or there, but when it comes down to it, Kim is the dessert chef. Here are a couple of recipes that have gone over really well. . .

Stout Cake

Yes, you read that correctly. There are constructive things you can do with beer *besides* drink it.

Cake →

½ Cup unsalted butter
1 ⅓ Cups dark brown sugar
2 Medium eggs, beaten
6 Ounces flour
¼ Tsp. baking powder
1 Tsp. baking soda
7 Ounces stout**
¼ Cup cocoa powder
**If you do not want to use stout, any dark cola may be substituted!

Icing→

4 Ounces chocolate
2 Tbsp. stout
2 Ounces unsalted butter
4 Ounces powdered sugar

Preheat oven to 350°

Grease and flour two 8 inch cake pans

Cream together butter and sugar, then beat in the eggs

In a separate bowl, sift together the baking powder, baking soda, and flour

Stir the stout into the cocoa (be careful here, as they do not mix well, at first)

Fold the flour and cocoa into the butter and sugar mixture, alternating a little of each at a time

Spread the batter into the pans and bake for 30 minutes, or until a toothpick inserted comes out clean

Cool the cakes while making the icing:

Melt the chocolate into the stout, then add the butter (beat it in)

Allow it to cool a bit, and then add the powdered sugar

When both cake and icing have cooled to a workable temperature, sandwich the cake with icing, and then ice the outside.

I rather enjoy this cake, as it is not nearly as sweet as some store-bought mixes. Don't be disappointed if, the first time you make this, it turns out a bit flat. The trick is to not let the stout (or soda) go too flat before pouring the batter and jamming it in the oven.

Chocolate Cement Pie

Don't let the name put you off; this pie is *excellent*, but it does feel like you've been bludgeoned with a chocolate-flavored cinder block if you have too much. This pie is *rich* and *very thick*. To date, I think we've burned up three blenders in the process of making it.

2 eggs
½ Cup melted butter
⅓ Cup flour
1 Cup chocolate chips
1 Cup chopped nuts (any are good, but I like pecans)
1 Cup sugar
1 Tbsp. bourbon (may be substituted with 1 Tsp. vanilla)
Pinch of salt
1 Uncooked pie crust
Whipped cream

In a blender or food processor, beat the eggs until they become frothy, then add the remaining ingredients and process until the nuts are finely chopped.

Pour into a pie shell and bake at 350° for 30-35 minutes or until the center rises and the pastry is tan.

Apple Bake

This recipe is simple, relatively quick, and can be easily done in a Dutch oven in the campfire, also.

Topping→

⅔ Cup all-purpose flour
⅓ Cup rolled oats
3 Tbsp. brown sugar
½ Cup Butter

Filling→

4 or 5 large apples
2 Tbsp. brown sugar
1 Tsp. cinnamon

Preheat the oven to 425° and grease a 2-quart baking dish.

Mix the topping ingredients in a large bowl.

Peel, core and slice the apples, then layer them in the baking dish. Sprinkle brown sugar and cinnamon over the slices, then sprinkle the topping mixture over the top.

Bake until the apples have softened and the topping is golden, about 20-25 minutes.

--If the topping begins to brown before the apples have finished cooking, cover the baking dish with foil and reduce the temperature to 350°--

Unusual Uses for Usual Items

As every adventurer is well aware, common items can have multiple uses. PVC pipe can be used for projects other than plumbing, paracord can be used for much more than merely lashing and binding, and don't get me started on everything you can use a bar of soap for. In the same manner, everyday items from your spice cabinet have uses beyond cooking. Keep in mind that people have allergies to herbs and spices. Be mindful of those around you if you decide to try these or any other alternative use items.

This is by no means a complete list, but here are a few of the more popular alternative applications:

- **Basil**—Hung, dried, in windows and on doors as a natural flying insect repellant.
- **Bay Leaves**—Acts as a repellant for moths and those little, wormy things that sometimes get into your dry goods. Place leaves in your flour, cereal, and rice containers.
- **Black Pepper**—When added to wash loads (by the teaspoon), black pepper will help keep colors from fading.
- **Cayenne Pepper**—A mixture of cayenne and water, when sprayed on the garden, will keep rabbits from feasting on your cabbages.
- **Cinnamon**—Boil cinnamon sticks to naturally freshen the air in the house (works for covering pet odors). Some ants are repelled by a mixture of cinnamon essential oil and water.
- **Cloves**—Cloves repel moths and smell better than mothballs.
- **Cream of Tartar**—A staple for the baking enthusiast, cream of tartar is also an excellent cleaning product. Mix ¼ cup C of T with 1 cup vinegar to polish stainless steel. Mix it with Hydrogen Peroxide into a thick paste to clean bath tubs and bathroom sinks. A ratio of 1:1 Cream of Tartar and Baking powder makes a gentle scouring powder for countertops and stovetops.
- **Lavender**—My grandmother used to use lavender oil on a cotton ball to keep flies away from the door. I'm not sure if it was any more than just marginally effective, but it did smell nice.
- **Mint**—Mint attracts beneficial insects to your garden while repelling a number of harmful ones. The essential oil is also good for repelling ants. Chewing the leaves is an excellent breath freshener (assuming the dog didn't have alternative intent for your mint bed, as well).
- **Turmeric**—One thing about turmeric is its ability to stain. It will stain your skin, if you get it on you. This does, however, make it a good choice for giving fabric an aged look, and it also makes a good Easter egg dye.

I'm going to be honest with everyone—this book was born from laziness. I was sitting in my kitchen one Saturday, waiting for Kim to come home from work and wondering what would be good for dinner. At the time, all of my recipes were contained on handwritten notes loosely tucked into sheet protectors in a portfolio-style binder that was an absolute *nightmare* to go through. Most of those notes were on post-its, scrap papers, even *napkins*, as every one of them happened on the fly, sometimes at home, sometimes in a campground. In a fit,

I tried to organize it, when the thought occurred to me, *why not just put it all in one, big file*? Later that night (dinner was Beef Burgundy, by the way), I had just started to organize everything when I had an epiphany—*maybe someone else would be interested in some of this, as well*. Since then, the idea grew from a simple cookbook to the pages you have before you today. I've had my shares of highs and lows over the years, testing everything herein on patient friends and family. Not everything was a home run, but as picky as some children are, a quick trot to first can be more than just a small victory. Here's hoping that you find adventure with family, good food, and great friends.

--Bob